Der, Die, Das

The Secrets of German Gender

**Constantin
Vayenas**

Constantin Vayenas
Der, Die, Das: The Secrets of German Gender

A catalogue record of this book is available from the Swiss National Library in the catalogue Schweizer Buch (www.nb.admin.ch).

ISBN 978-3-9524810-0-4

Additional information and contact details:

www.der-die-das.ch

Table of Contents

Introduction

Foreigners wishing to speak German well, face the confidence-sapping challenge that they usually don't know the gender of many nouns. Given that nouns typically constitute over seventy per cent of the words in the German language, [1] this is not an insignificant hurdle. If we then consider that the articles – *der, die, das* – collectively, are the most frequently-used words in the German language, [2] the inability to correctly map enough of them to sound fluent can be annoying. Even though foreign students might have invested many hours into their German, they know that using the wrong gender sounds uneducated and distracts the listener from the key message.

Why is it so difficult for foreign students to master German gender? There are two key reasons: First, it is not taught. German grammar books avoid it. In the same way that German grammar books are not dictionaries and do not define words, they do not see it as their task to explain the relationship between nouns and gender. That's someone else's specialization, not theirs. [3] This approach of not teaching German gender to foreign students is exactly what Mark Twain experienced with his German teachers in the 19th century: "Every noun has a gender, and there is no sense or system in the distribution; so the gender of each must be learned separately and by heart. There is no other way." [4]

Essentially, then, foreign students trying to figure out German gender are told to memorize the dictionary. This tough-love message was informed by the view espoused by the likes of Twain's German teachers that the allocation of gender to nouns is essentially arbitrary. That being the case, they believed that there were no special insights on this topic that could be taught to foreign students of the language. [5]

But then came the computer age, with its ability to process vast amounts of data. Linguists started running the German dictionary through software and writing PhD theses on the results. This work has resulted in ground-breaking insights. [6] Their work showed that the link between gender and nouns did not appear to be quite so arbitrary. The more they analyzed, the more patterns they discovered.

Their important findings have *not*, however, been incorporated into standard German grammar books because, as mentioned earlier, this topic is not viewed as falling within the scope of standard grammar. This omission, in turn, means that these insights are not known by German language teachers and, therefore, are not taught to those who would benefit the most from this knowledge, namely, foreign students of German. It's not that German language teachers don't know when to map *der*, *die* or *das* to a noun – they obviously do know that – it's just that they were never taught the principles that determine gender. That's a very different subject. That's like knowing the history of words. Very few of us know the history of words. If we had to explain to someone who is learning English why "gh" is pronounced "f" in "cough" but is silent in "dough", we wouldn't be able to do it. We just know how to write those words and how to pronounce them, and that's all we ever needed to know. It's the same for native German speakers: they don't know the *why* of gender, so they can't explain it to us. Their message to us is: "Don't ask why, just memorize it."

This brings us to the second reason why it is so difficult for foreign students to master German gender: If they aren't taught the principles that determine the gender of nouns in grammar books, they need to acquire this knowledge by some other way. That would be the same way that German children learnt it, namely, through immersion. That was so easy. By the age of two, German children are already making a distinction between the gender of German nouns, with a preference for using the indefinite article (*ein/eine*) rather than the definite article (*der/die/das*).[7] By the age of five their mastery of German gender is pretty good, but they tend to avoid or leave out the definite article in cases where they don't know what it should be. By the age of seven, in tests using fake nouns to see how they will react, German children tend to allocate the same gender to those fake words that adults do when they take the test.[8] And by the time that they've reached the age of ten, German children have essentially mastered German gender.

The German brain has, therefore, been programmed to assign a gender to German nouns, based on years of exposure. They don't know why their brain comes up with allocating a gender to fake words, which is the same gender that most of the others are also selecting – they just do it. They can't explain what determines gender, they just know it.

This book familiarizes you, the foreign student of German, with the *what*, the *why* and the *how* of gender, i.e. with the "coding" by which the German brain selects gender for fake words. The approach used is one of reverse engineering: If you know what determines the gender of German nouns, then you have a better chance of identifying the correct gender of a new or unfamiliar noun. Be warned, though: This is definitely not how Germans learnt the gender of their nouns – they were never required to know the "coding" that determined why a girl, *Mädchen*, is not feminine. This is not what native German speakers were taught at home or in their grammar books at school. But since you didn't get the exposure that they got as a child, not to speak of the many further hours after that, and since you don't now want to arbitrarily memorize the gender of every noun in the dictionary, the next best thing is to take a look at this "coding". Its two main principles are that German gender has been shaped by *categories* and *sounds*.

Rule 1: Categories

Nouns for *similar categories of things or concepts* tend to have the same gender. Thus, colours and the names of medicines and chemicals tend to be neuter, numbers and the names of flowers and fruit tend to be feminine, and seasons, days and months are masculine. By knowing, for example, that almost all drinks are masculine, you have the password to unlock the gender of a cappuccino, a Rooibos tea, a Merlot wine and an apple juice.[9]

Given the importance of categories for determining gender, when new things are invented, the new nouns tend to take the gender of words with a similar meaning. For example, when the mobile phone was invented, it became *das Handy* because it belonged to the same category as *das Telefon*.

Categories are a hugely relevant identifier of gender. So much so, that one can even identify certain attributes that are unique to each gender.

Neuter tends to be the category for many of the most fundamental elements of nature (atoms, molecules, electrons, neutrons, and life itself, *das Leben*). Not surprisingly, therefore, neuter includes almost all elements in the Periodic Table. Neuter's association with physics is revealed by some of the things it measures: *das Ampere, das Ohm, das Watt, das Volt, das Newton, das Celsius, das Fahrenheit, das Kelvin, das Kilogramm.*

Neuter is also the gender for higher levels of classification of physical things, like "the universe" or "the animal". A neuter noun thus often stands at the top of the pyramid of its subject matter, like *das Tier*, followed by the individual nouns for each member of the animal kingdom. It's almost as if, first came neuter, and then everything else.

Another way to think about this is in terms of Venn diagrams – those circles we learnt at school. If we were to apply Venn diagrams to German gender, neuter will typically be the outer circle, which contains everything else.

As can be seen from Exhibit 1, while neuter typically represents the largest circle of its category, the subcomponents inside can consist of many different things, each with their own gender, including, again, neuter.

Exhibit 1: Visualizing how neuter is the gender for the largest collection of things

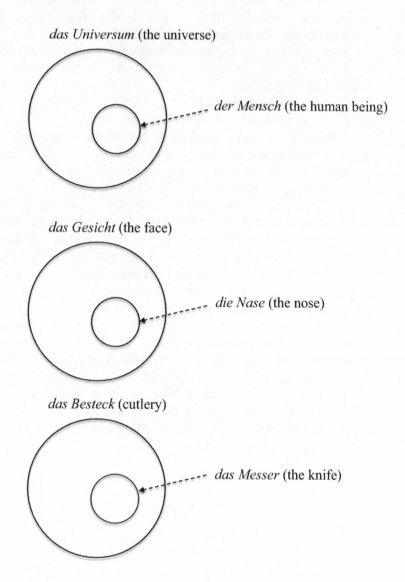

das Universum (the universe)

der Mensch (the human being)

das Gesicht (the face)

die Nase (the nose)

das Besteck (cutlery)

das Messer (the knife)

Neuter also has other characteristics. It has a powerful role over all nouns in that it is the default gender for the diminutive. When John becomes little Johnny, that would change him to neuter in German: *das Hänschen klein, das Büblein*. For the same reason, even a little girl is neuter: *das Mädchen*.

The ability of neuter to harmonize the gender of nouns is also seen in its power over many foreign nouns imported into German. Knowing this, one can unlock the German gender of *Jogging, Tennis, Poker* and *Croissant* – they're all *das*.

When an imported foreign word is not neuter, then this is usually because a German synonym already exists for it in another gender.[10] Categories are for simplification, and the simplest thing is to put the imported word into its existing category.

Neuter also has the unique quality that it is the gender of last resort – the default for "the", "that", "this", "it" – without being more specific. For example, you could say "Was ist denn *das*?" or "*es* hat mich gefreut", even when referring to a thing, person or situation of any gender, because it fudges what, specifically, you are referring to, even if it might be kind of implicit. But the moment you specify the noun, the neuter fudge becomes a blunt instrument and you have to map the noun to its gender.

Let's move on to the characteristics of feminine and masculine nouns. They are different.

Feminine is the gender *of almost half* the nouns in German.[11] Given this high ratio, we could basically say that, statistically, German nouns are either feminine or something else: about thirty per cent are masculine and around twenty per cent are neuter. In fact, feminine is so dominant a gender that when five-year-old German children make mistakes in selecting the gender of a noun, they tend to over-use *die* – a clear sign that they are hearing it more often than *der* and *das*.[12]

If neuter has a strong connection to the physical world, feminine tends to be the gender for the more abstract. Feminine is the gender of numbers, mathematics, certain shapes, certain behaviours, logic, love and even magic. The connection to numbers grants the feminine gender the power to turn single nouns into plural concepts, which is why *die Mannschaft* is singular and feminine, even though it could also refer to a male team.

What, precisely, differentiates nouns by gender has intrigued those looking for answers. When, in the late 1800s, German linguists started publishing research about the distinctions between feminine and masculine nouns, they inevitably started with the evidence as far back as they could find: an analysis of the gender of Greek and Latin nouns. [13] Like German, those ancient languages also have three genders, and they had an impact on German.

Why, for example, should the German word for hunting, *Jagd*, be feminine? From the time that they lived in caves, wasn't hunting the job of the male species? Even in modern times, isn't this stereotypically a male activity?

In looking for possible answers from the ancient Greeks and the Romans, some interesting patterns emerge. Was it just a coincidence that both the Greeks and the Romans had a female goddess of hunting, Artemis and Diana? Even if hunting was a man's job, a man could return empty-handed with no food for the family. One, therefore, had to respect the goddess of hunting – she oversaw *die Jagd*. She was there in the wild (*die Wildnis*) during the search (*die Suche*) for food (*die Nahrung, die Speise, die Kost*). She helped when darkness fell (*die Finsternis*), and when you had to make a quick escape (*die Flucht*) from danger (*die Gefahr*). Given all that power (*die Macht*), it seems that hunting had to be feminine!

Possibly in a similar way, the early generations didn't want to fool around with the male gods of war, wine, wealth, sleep, dreams, the sky, the ocean, the wind and death – *der Krieg, der Wein, der Reichtum, der Schlaf, der Traum, der Himmel, der Ozean, der Wind, der Tod.* And for the same reason, it was safer to acknowledge the female goddesses of love, beauty, wisdom, justice, force, the night, magic, art, science, poetry, music, tragedy, hymns, comedy and astronomy – *die Liebe, die Schönheit, die Weisheit, die Gerechtigkeit, die Gewalt, die Nacht, die Magie, die Kunst, die Wissenschaft, die Poesie, die Musik, die Tragödie, die Hymne, die Komödie, die Sternkunde.*

Of course, the Germanic tribes also had their differentiating experiences. Despite the Greeks and Romans having a male sun god, and the word "sun" remaining masculine to this very day in Greek, Italian, French, Spanish and Portuguese, the Germans opted for a feminine noun: *die Sonne*. Could this have been because of the Germanic sun goddess, Sunna, whose brother is the moon, *der Mond*?

Wisdom is a feminine noun in both Greek and Latin, and is treated as a feminine concept in English in the Bible: "Yet wisdom is justified by *her* deeds." (Matthew 11:19). The Greek noun for wisdom is "sophia", and *love of sophia*, philosophy, is feminine in both Greek and German. Perhaps not too surprisingly, therefore, knowledge and wisdom are a feminine category in German too. Also think of the blindfolded Lady Justice. Hence, we have: *die Art, die Besonnenheit, die Bildung, die Einsicht, die Gerechtigkeit, die Intelligenz, die Justiz, die Kenntnis, die Klugheit, die Kunst, die Methode, die Methodik, die Philosophie, die Ratio, die Sorgfalt, die Technik, die Technologie, die Umsicht, die Vorausschau, die Voraussicht, die Vorsicht, die Vernunft, die Weise, die Weisheit, die Weitsicht.*

Further study into the differences between the characteristics of feminine and masculine German nouns reveal that feminine abstract nouns tend to refer to more submissive aspects, whereas masculine abstract nouns represent more aggressive concepts.[14]

Courage (*der Mut*), disdainfulness (*der Hochmut*), over-confidence (*der Übermut*), and error (*der Irrtum*) are masculine. In contrast, the nouns one might associate with Cinderella are feminine: humility (*die Demut*), patience (*die Geduld*), kindness (*die Gutherzigkeit*), and, alas, poverty (*die Armut*). Poverty can lead to a lot of worry: *die Angst, die Sorge, die Besorgnis.* But let's also not forget the nouns for Cinderella's step-sisters: jealousy (*die Eifersucht*), ugliness (*die Hässlichkeit*), abuse (*die Misshandlung*), cruelty (*die Grausamkeit*) and meanness (*die Gemeinheit*).

The feminine gender is where the real power resides, though: *die Kraft, die Macht, die Leistung, die Energie, die Stärke, die Festigkeit, die Belastbarkeit, die Gewalt, die Befugnis* (authorization), *die Wucht* (impact), *die Potenz, die Mächtigkeit, die Herrschaft* (dominion), *die Vollmacht* (power of attorney), *die Behörde, die Autorität, die Regierung, die Kontrolle* (supervision), *die Steuerung* (governance).

In contrast, masculine power appears more physically overt. In the animal world, large scary animals tend to be masculine: *der Dinosaurier, der Elefant, der Gorilla, der Orang-Utan*, whereas smaller, less scary animals (*die Maus*) or more elegant animals (*die Giraffe*) tend to be feminine. This is an indication that gender is also a reflection of form and shape.

Elongated shapes tend to be masculine, such as arrows (*der Pfeil*), poles (*der Pfahl*), pillars and columns (*der Pfeiler*), posts (*der Pfosten*), masts (*der Mast*), staffs and rods (*der Stab*), sticks (*der Stecken*), canes (*der Stock*), tree trunks (*der Stamm*) and stems (*der Stiel*). In contrast, flat surfaces tend to be feminine: walls, doors, ceilings, blackboards, plains, etc. – *die Fläche, die Ebene, die Wand, die Mauer, die Tafel, die Decke, die Tür, die Seite, die Flanke, die Platte*. Hollow objects also tend to be feminine: boxes, tins, cans, caves, drums, pipes, tubes – *die Büchse, die Box, die Dose, die Höhle, die Schachtel, die Trommel, die Tube, die Röhre*. And sharp shapes (needles, forks, pliers, scissors, claws and hooks) tend to be feminine: *die Nadel, die Gabel, die Zange, die Schere, die Klaue, die Kralle, die Pratze*.

Like an inheritance divided up between sons and daughters, the boys got a big chunk of the sky: the heavens, planets, moons and stars; in contrast, the girls got the sun, the earth and the planet Venus.

When a German noun looks like it should fit into a category, but doesn't, then one might need to think about the possibility that the category in question might be structured like a continuum or a hierarchy. Let's take the example of time; the shortest intervals of time are feminine: *die Zeit, die Uhr, die Stunde, die Minute, die Sekunde*; the longest time-periods are neuter: *das Jahr, das Jahrzehnt* (decade), *das Jahrhundert* (century), *das Jahrtausend* (millenium), and the periods in-between are masculine: *der Tag, der Monat*. When a noun still doesn't appear to fit into its category, as in the case of *die Woche, die Dekade, die Epoche*, then one needs to use the other key to unlock the mystery: *sounds*.

Rule 2: Sounds

Nouns that start with certain letters, end in certain letters or have a similar nasal or vowel sound tend to have the same gender. This is a continuation of the concept of categories: similar things get allocated to the same gender. All of this categorization serves just one single purpose: to facilitate communication between those of the same tribe. This is about clarity and survival. When, in a candle-lit kitchen from the Dark Ages, you ask someone to pass you a spoon, you don't want them handing over a knife.

Using the right gender is going to make doubly sure that you communicate accurately. Hence it is perhaps not too surprising to see that nouns of a certain sound tend to be associated with a particular gender. Nouns ending on *-e* are feminine 90 per cent of the time, those ending on *-ie* are feminine 95 per cent of the time, *-ur* nouns are feminine 93 per cent, *-ucht* endings are feminine 64 per cent, *-ich* masculine 81 per cent, *-ett* neuter 95 per cent, and *-ier* neuter 60 per cent of the time.[15]

Let's apply this. If you had to try and identify the gender of *Spur* (track/lane/trail), knowing that nouns ending on *-ur* are feminine 93 per cent of the time has essentially handed you the answer. If you still wanted to try and go for an even higher level of certainty, you could see if Rule 1 (categories) offers any help. Which nouns mean the same thing as a track, lane or trail? *Die Strasse, die Allee, die Route, die Bahn, die Autobahn, die Piste, die Schiene, die Strecke*. That seems even clearer. That list of feminine nouns overwhelms two masculine synomyms: *der Weg, der Pfad*. You'd stand a good chance, therefore, if you opted for *die Spur*.

Thanks to the work of computer-age linguists,[16] we now know many more of the sound associations between nouns and gender. Thus, the more consonants at the beginning or end of the noun, the likelier that it is a masculine noun, especially if the noun has only one syllable. The probability that nouns modelled on the following single-syllable examples, which start and end on a consonant, is masculine, is 83 per cent: *Schlaf, Sand, Zwerg, Knall, Drall, Schlamm*. Think of male teenagers giving you one-syllable answers, and you now know that most such short nouns are masculine.

And then there are endings that tend to be shared between just two genders, which gives students a fifty per cent chance of being right. That fifty per cent chance can often be boosted further still, by also drawing on clues from Rule 1 (categories). For example, nouns ending on *-nis* are either feminine or neuter. Knowing that neuter is more likely to be the gender of inanimate objects and feminine the gender of the more abstract, helps students to guess the gender of the nouns *Gefängnis* (prison, an inanimate object) and *Bedrängnis* (distress, an abstract concept). The assumption that it is probably *das Gefängnis* could have been boosted further by the knowledge that nouns starting with *Ge-* tend to be neuter. Here we see the interplay of several signals helping one guess the correct gender: The noun starts with *Ge-* (a strong neuter signal) and it ends on *-nis* (a signal that it could be neuter if it is an inanimate object). Using the same principle, namely that a noun ending on *-nis* is likely to be feminine if it represents an abstract concept, we would not be wrong if we opted for *die Bedrängnis*.

Let's take another example from the *-nis* category: You need to guess the gender of *Kenntnis* (knowledge) and *Zeugnis* (reference). The former is abstract, the latter something more concrete, typically a piece of paper: therefore, it is probably *die Kenntnis* and *das Zeugnis*. Of course, these distinctions will not always be that obvious, but the more aware one is of the "coding" on which the allocation of grammatical gender in German is built, the more useful it becomes every time one encounters new nouns that fit the patterns one knows or recognizes. Simply being aware of this "coding" is valuable, therefore, because you'll keep looking for the evidence. And when a noun you encounter doesn't fit into an existing pattern, you'll want to know why and you'll have the confidence to look for solutions, because you now know that the allocation of gender is not as arbitrary as Twain was taught.

Let's try another example. You have to guess the gender of three nouns, and you are told that each has a different gender: *Gier* (greed), *Atelier* (a studio), *Stier* (a bull). In this case, Rule 2 is not of much help because all three nouns have the exact same ending. You try to see if Rule 1 might offer clues: feminine for the more abstract, neuter for the inanimate, and masculine for what is probably masculine if it is a living thing. You won't be wrong, therefore, if you guessed *die Gier, das Atelier, der Stier.*

As you become more aware of the connection between German nouns and categories, you'll discover overlapping categories and additional possibilities to help unlock their gender. Think of those Venn diagrams referred to earlier and let's take the noun *Atelier* again. It is a French word, and foreign nouns imported into German tend to become neuter, hence it is probably *das Atelier*. Or, *Atelier* is in the same category of things as *das Haus, das Zimmer, das Studio, das Gebäude, das Geschäft*, which increases the probability that it will also likely be *das Atelier*.[17] The more you begin to think of German nouns in terms of categories, the more possibilities you will find to guess the correct gender (Exhibit 2).

Exhibit 2: How overlapping gender categories can provide clues to the gender of nouns

Category X: imported nouns tend to be neuter

Category Y: synonyms of *das Haus, das Zimmer, das Studio* are also likely to be neuter

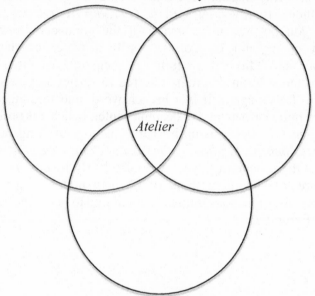

Atelier

Category Z: nouns ending on *-ier* tend to be neuter if they refer to inanimate objects

Rule 1 and Rule 2 sometimes work in perfect harmony with each other, in which case you have a double confirmation that your guess is right. But, there are also clashes between these rules that you need to be aware of. Rule 1 (categories) tends to be more powerful than rule 2 (sounds). Thus, the category "rivers in central Europe" tends to be feminine (*die Donau*), and "rivers outside of central Europe" tends to be masculine (*der Nil*), regardless of the sounds associated with their names. But there are also cases where a particular sound (Rule 2) is so strongly associated with a particular gender, that it always overpowers Rule 1. For example, the ending *-erei* is almost always feminine, no matter what the category might suggest the gender of a particular noun should be. That's then a pretty strong signal that, for those nouns, Rule 2 will probably lead. Let's take an example of Rule 2 (sounds) beating Rule 1 (categories). We already know that the more consonants a noun has at the beginning and the end, the likelier that it is masculine. This is the case with *Pfirsich* (peach). While the category "fruit" is overwhelmingly feminine, this particular noun is simply too cluttered with consonants to be in the feminine club: it is *der Pfirsich*. Rule 2 wins.

When an ending does not appear to fit a rule, other factors might be at work. For example, it might be that the noun is an abbreviation, because abbreviations and acronyms take the gender of their respective full word: thus, *die Lokomotive*, which ends on the feminine *-e*, is abbreviated as *die Lok*, which has no feminine *-e* to it, and whose gender would stump you if you came across it for the first time.

Some of the exceptions appear to have no modern-day rhyme or reason to them, such as why a knife, a fork and a spoon – the most basic and important of kitchen table utensils – should each have a different gender in German.

Let's start with the knife: metals tend to be neuter and weapons tend to be neuter. A sword (*das Schwert*), a long metal blade used for cutting, is neuter. Should we, therefore, be terribly surprised that *das Messer,* a small metal blade used for cutting, should also be neuter? One down, two to go: the fork. This is a more lady-like way to eat. Marie Antoinette did not remove her gloves when eating; she used a fork. The German noun for fork, *Gabel*, at different times used to have both a feminine *-a* ending and a feminine *-e* ending. Of course, that's not something an ordinary person would know today. But the point is that the gender of nouns is not a totally arbitrary phenomenon. Every noun has a history and a context – we just don't typically know that history or context. The word *Gabel* is also linked to the same German category as *die Forke* (a garden fork or a pitchfork). There is also another relevant overlapping category: "sharp shapes" tend to be feminine, as in *die Nadel* (needle). [18] So, with that extensive pedigree, it does not seem unreasonable that the fork should be feminine: *die Gabel*.

This leaves us with the spoon. If using the fork is to eat lady-like, then slurping with a spoon is less so. The spoon has rougher associations; it is masculine: *der Löffel*.

Now that you know the background to their gender, the association might stick: *das Messer, die Gabel, der Löffel*. Even if you remember just one of the three stories, you've reached a one hundred per cent probability that you will always recall the right gender for the one utensil whose story you do remember.

This still leaves the key question *Why*? What is the purpose of three genders? Why not just go for one? If English can manage with only "the", why does German need so many?

The general assumption is that for something to survive over so many centuries, it must have value. The key role of German gender appears to be for *precision*. Anybody who has ever tried to do some serious translation from English into German will know that German, the language of Einstein, tends to be far more precise than English. Translating the English word "it" into German would immediately require the German writer to determine whether that means "er", "sie", "es", "ihn", "ihm", "ihr", "der", "die" or "das". A higher degree of precision is arguably also more important in German than in English, because German sentences tend to be a lot longer than English ones (around twenty per cent longer) and German sentences tend to have the verb at the end of the sentence, far from the subject. Avoiding confusion about who did what to whom, with what and when, needs more precise identifiers when sentences are longer and the verb is separated from the subject by many other words. This strongly suggests that the Germans are not going to abandon gender any time soon.[19]

How should this guide be used? You might want to first read through the guide, as you would a book, and then return to specific sections to reinforce their relevance to you. As you become more aware of Rules 1 and 2, they'll help you unlock the gender of entire categories of nouns, thereby boosting your confidence in speaking German. The purpose of bringing in many examples is to try and make the rule more memorable by increasing the likelihood that you will find nouns that strengthen your association to a particular rule.

The Index at the back also serves as the basis to test yourself. Each entry can be used as a question: "What gender does this entry tend to represent?" Remember, that you are dealing with probabilities. The more you combine your knowledge from Rules 1 and 2, the higher you raise the probability that you will guess the correct gender.

The key value of this book is to illustrate the patterns that link nouns to a particular gender. You might, therefore, want to try jotting down such new nouns that you discover fit the patterns. It is also likely that you will discover new categories and new interconnections that are relevant for the vocabularly that you require in your field of expertise. More discoveries are waiting to be made.

Given how much you have probably already invested in your German to reach this point, unlocking gender through reverse engineering is an adventure that you will probably enjoy a lot. A word of warning, though. Native German speakers, unless they are professors of German linguistics with a specialization in the esoteric topic of grammatical gender, are unlikely to share your excitement that you have discovered the keys to determining gender. To them, gender is a no-brainer – all easy-peasy stuff. And since they were never taught reverse-engineering gender tools at school, they'll be sceptical that you are learning "rules" they've never heard of. And as you become more expert at this and want to talk about it, they might humour you for a bit, but they'll soon tire of you trying to teach them the principles that govern the gender of their own language. To them this is all pointless – they can already do it without even having to think. They don't know the *why*, just the *how*. You're learning the *why* so that you can know the *how*.

So, for motivation, share your excitement with fellow students who are struggling, like you, to master German gender.

Der: The rules that make nouns masculine

Rule 1: Categories

Many types of animals: (especially if they are bigger, scarier, uglier, or more powerful, or appear as the villains in fairy tales) der Adler, der Alligator, der Bär, der Biber, der Blauwal, der Büffel, der Delphin, der Dinosaurier, der Elefant, der Esel, der Fisch, der Fuchs, der Gorilla, der Hahn, der Hummer, der Hund, der Löwe, der Maulwurf, der Orang-Utan, der Stier, der Tiger, der Vogel, der Wal, der Wolf. If the animals are smaller and less powerful, they can usually be identified as being male if they end on *-er*: der Hamster, der Käfer

Times of the day: der Morgen, der Abend, der Mittag (but not *die Nacht*, because nouns ending on *-acht* tend to be feminine)

Days of the week: der Tag, der Montag, der Dienstag, der Mittwoch, der Donnerstag, etc.

Months: der Monat, der Januar, der Februar, der März, etc.

Seasons: der Frühling, der Sommer, der Herbst, der Winter

Points on the compass: der Norden, der Süden, der Osten, der Westen, der Nordosten, der Pol, der Nordpol, der Südpol, der Gegenpol, der Kompass

Precipitation and wind: der Tropfen, der Regen, der Nebel, der Schnee, der Hagel, der Sturm, der Blitz, der Donner, der Wind, der Tornado, der Hurrikan, der Föhn, der Passat, etc.
(Exceptions: *die Böe, die Brise, die Bise* – because they end on *-e*, which is associated with feminine nouns)

Heavenly bodies: der Asteroid, der Jupiter, der Himmel, der Komet, der Mars, der Merkur, der Mond, der Neptun, der Planet, der Quasar, der Pluto, der Pulsar, der Satellit, der Saturn, der Stern; Venus is both the Roman goddess of love and the name of a planet, hence feminine, and *die Sonne* and *die Erde* both have the powerful *-e* ending, typically associated with feminine nouns.

Types of soil, minerals and rock: der Boden, der Stein, der Fels, der Granit, der Diamant, der Marmor, der Quarz, der Sand, der Smaragd (emerald). Exception: *die Kreide* (chalk, ending on the feminine *-e*)

Dirt & waste: der Abfall, der Dreck, der Dung, der Kehricht der Plunder (junk), der Mist, der Müll, der Schmuddel, der Schrott, der Staub, der Schmutz, der Urin, etc.

Names of many rivers outside of central Europe: der Amazonas, der Mississippi, der Nil (exceptionally also *der Rhein, der Main*).

Inland bodies of water: der Bach (stream), der Fluss (from which we also get several related masculine nouns: der Abfluss, der Ausfluss, der Einfluss), der Kanal (channel), der See (lake), der Teich (pond), der Damm (dam), der Pool/der Swimmingpool[20]

Names of mountains: der Berg, der Gipfel, der Hügel, der Mount Everest, der Mont Blanc, der Kilimanjaro – even in the case of *der Himalaja/der Himalaya*, which ends on an *-a*, which tends to be a feminine ending.[21]

Elongated shapes:

- o der Arm (arm/sleeve/branch/limb)
- o der Ast (branch)
- o der Baumstamm (tree trunk)
- o der Draht (wire)
- o der Golfschläger (golf club)
- o der Hals/der Nacken (neck)
- o der Mast (mast/pylon)
- o der Pfahl (pole/stake)
- o der Pfeiler (pillar/column)
- o der Pfosten (post)
- o der Schenkel (leg/thigh/geometric side)
- o der Stab (staff/rod)
- o der Stecken (stick)
- o der Stiel (stalk/stem)
- o der Stift (pen/pencil)
- o der Stock (stick/cane)
- o der Turm (tower)

Cloth: der Filz (felt), der Lappen (cloth/rag), der Stoff (material/cloth/fabric), der Taft (taffeta, woven silk or similar synthetic fabric)

Types of fish: der Fisch, der Aal (eel), der Lachs (salmon), der Kabeljau (cod), der Haifisch (shark), der Barsch (bass), der Thunfisch (tuna). Exceptions: when the noun ends on the feminine -e: *die Forelle* (trout), *die Seezunge* (sole)

Plants: With the exception of trees, flowers and fruit (which tend to be feminine, especially if they end on an -e), plants, vegetables, salads and spices tend to be masculine if they don't end on -e: der Bambus (bamboo), der Brokkoli, der Blumenkohl (cauliflower), der Fenchel (fennel), der Rosenkohl (Brussels sprouts), der Spinat (spinach), der Pfeffer (pepper), der Hanf (cannabis), der Lauch (leek), der Pilz (mushroom), der Meerrettich (horseradish), der Ingwer (ginger), der Senf (mustard), der Oregano, der Schnittlauch, der Dill, der Thymian, der Estragon, der Rosmarin, der Koriander, der Salat, der Reis, der Mais

Juices: der Saft, der Apfelsaft, der Orangensaft, der Zitronensaft

Coffee, tea and cake: der Tee (→ der Rooibos), der Kaffee (→ der Espresso, der Cappuccino), der Kuchen

Names of alcoholic beverages: der Alkohol, der Champagner, der Cognac, der Likör, der Ouzo, der Prosecco, der Rum, der Schnaps, der Sekt, der Wein, der Whiskey, der Wodka (exception: *das Bier*[22])

Subcategories take the same gender as the main category:

- der Wein → der Merlot, der Spätburgunder
- der Cocktail → der Mojito, der Cosmopolitan
- das Bier → das Pils (a type of beer)

Equipment/instruments/tools: (especially when these nouns end on *-er* or *-or*)

- der Atomreaktor
- der Computer
- der Cursor
- der Detektor
- der Fernseher
- der Generator
- der Katalysator
- der Kondensator
- der Kugelschreiber
- der Monitor
- der Motor
- der Projektor
- der Prozessor
- der Radiator

- der Sensor
- der Simulator
- der Stabilisator
- der Taschenrechner
- der Toaster
- der Traktor
- der Ventilator

Some non-equipment nouns ending on -*or*:

- der Chor (choir)
- der Faktor
- der Horror
- der Humor
- der Indikator
- der Korridor
- der Sektor
- der Terror
- der Tresor
- der Tumor
- der Vektor

Names of car brands: der Audi, der BMW, der Mercedes, der Volkswagen, etc., tend to be masculine. This rule does not extend to car types. Hence it is *das Cabriolet* (a car with a roof that folds down) and *das Coupé* (a car with a fixed roof and two doors), because these nouns are of French origin, and nouns imported into German tend to become neuter. It is *die Limousine*, though, because it has the feminine -*e* ending.

Names of trains: der Zug, der ICE, der TGV

Many currencies: Der US-Dollar, der Euro, der Schweizer Franken, der südafrikanische Rand, der Renminbi, der chinesische Yuan, der japanische Yen, der Rubel, der Peso, der Cent, der Pfennig, der Rappen

Exceptions: das britische Pfund (because the pound as a measure of weight is neuter), die Lira, die Krone (because they end on -*a* or -*e*), die Mark, die Deutschmark, die D-Mark (which used to have either an -*a* and -*e* ending to it in the Middle Ages)

Types of music: der Blues, der Jazz, der Pop, der Rock, der Rap, der Reggae, der Schlager (but apparently not the more established varieties: die Klassik, die Oper)

Types of dances: der Foxtrott, der Tango, der Bolero, der Flamenco, der Cha-Cha-Cha, der Mambo, der Rumba, der Samba,[23] der Walzer. Exceptions: die Polka, das Menuett

Nouns that denote masculine persons tend to be masculine: This should be the most intuitive category, of course, but is not always so in the case of German. While there is a connection between the "natural gender" of the person and the "grammatical gender" of the noun in the case of *der Mann, der Vater, der Sohn, der Bub, der Bruder, der Onkel*, etc., diminutive forms change the gender to neuter, as in *das Bübchen*, the little boy, or *das Männchen* (when referring to a little man, perhaps more out of pity or as a caricature). There are also several instances where, even when we are referring to a male person, the gender of the noun is not necessarily masculine, as in the case of *die Person* (the person) or *die Geisel* (the hostage).

Rule 2: Sounds

Masculine nouns tend to start and end on a consonant, and the more consonants there are at the beginning and the end of each noun, the likelier it is that the noun will be masculine.

Nouns with the prefixes and suffixes below are typically masculine:

-aal: der Aal (fish: eel), der Saal – hall, and its many derivatives: e.g., der Gerichtssaal (court room), der Speisesaal (dining hall), der Wartesaal (waiting room)

-ag:

- o der Airbag
- o der Alltag
- o der Anschlag
- o der Antrag
- o der Auftrag
- o der Beitrag
- o der Belag
- o der Durchschlag
- o der Ertrag
- o der Gag (from the English word gag)[24]
- o der Hag
- o der Jetlag
- o der Lag (from the English word lag)
- o der Montag
- o der Schlag
- o der Tag
- o der Verlag
- o der Vertrag
- o der Vorschlag

-all:

- o der Abfall
- o der Aufprall
- o der Ball
- o der Drall (spin/rotation)
- o der Fall
- o der Hall (echo)

- o der Knall
- o der Krawall
- o der Kristall
- o der Schall
- o der Vorfall
- o der Zufall

Exceptions (neuter):

- o das All (same category as *das Universum*)
- o das Intervall (originally from the Latin *intervallum*, which would make the imported noun neuter in German)
- o das Metall (metals tend to be neuter)

Exceptions (feminine): *die Nachtigall* (smaller birds tend to be feminine, as in the case of the nightingale)

-am: der Gram (grief), der Kram (stuff/clutter), der Imam, der Islam, der Sesam (sesame), der Poetry-Slam, der Grand Slam

-an: Nouns ending on *-an* tend to be masculine. The *-an* ending is so strong that it even overrules the usual principle that imported words tend to become neuter

- o der Altan (type of balcony)
- o der Baldrian (valerian plant or drug)
- o der Balkan (the Balkans)
- o der Blödian (idiot)
- o der Caravan (caravan)
- o der Dekan (dean)
- o der Diözesan (member of a diocese)
- o der Diwan (divan)
- o der Dressman (model for men's fashion)
- o der Elan (zeal/vigour)
- o der Enzian (gentian plant)
- o der Fan (admirer/supporter/fan)

- der Fasan (pheasant)
- der Gentleman
- der Grobian (ruffian/course person)
- der Grünspan (verdigris)
- der Hooligan
- der Hurrikan (hurricane)
- der Iran, der Sudan, der Südsudan (some of the few countries that are masculine – most are neuter)
- der Kaftan (caftan/kaftan)
- der Katamaran (catamaran)
- der Klan (clan)
- der Koran
- der Kran (crane)
- der Kumpan (pal/buddy)
- der Lebertran (cod liver oil)
- der Leguan (iguana)
- der Majoran (majoram: spices tend to be masculine)
- der Median (median)
- der Meridian (meridian)
- der Merlan (fish: whiting)
- der Orang-Utan (orangutan)
- der Orkan (gale-force wind)
- der Ortolan (bird: ortalan)
- der Ozean (ocean)
- der Parmesan (Parmesan cheese)
- der Pavian (baboon)
- der Pelikan (pelican)
- der Plan (plan)
- der Ramadan (Ramadan)
- der Roman (novel/work of fiction)
- der Safran (saffron: spices tend to be masculine)
- der Schlendrian (a person dragging their feet/an inefficient person)
- der Schwan (swan)
- der Slogan (slogan)
- der Sopran (soprano)
- der Span (splinter, wooden chip)

o der Steppenwaran (a type of lizzard)
o der Stuntman
o der Sultan
o der Talisman (talisman)
o der Tarzan
o der Thymian (thyme: spices tend to be masculine)
o der Titan (the Greek god/a strong person)
o der Tran (whale oil/train oil)
o der Tukan (bird: toucan)
o der Turban (turban)
o der Ulan (a horseman armed with a spear)
o der Untertan (a subject, in a monarchy)
o der Van (van/type of car)
o der Vatikan (Vatican)
o der Veteran (veteran)
o der Vulkan (volcano/Roman god of fire)
o der Yuan (the Chinese currency)

Several masculine names end on *-an*:

(der) Adrian, (der) Christian, (der) Fabian, (der) Florian, (der) Ivan, (der) Jean, (der) Jonathan, (der) Julian, (der) Kian, (der) Kilian, (der) Marian, (der) Maximilian, (der) Sebastian, (der) Stefan/Stephan, (der) Tilman, (der) Tristan

Exceptions: The names of countries tend to be neuter, and this also tends to be the case with names ending on *-an*:[25] (das) Afghanistan, (das) Aserbaidschan, (das) Bhutan, (das) Japan, (das) Kasachstan, (das) Kirgistan, (das) Kurdistan, (das) Pakistan, (das) Tadschikistan, (das) Taiwan, (das) Turkmenistan, (das) Usbekistan

Other neuter exceptions to the *-an* ending: Elements in the Periodic Table, metals, gasses, chemical substances and their derivatives tend to be neuter:

o das Butan (butane)

- o das Filigran (filigree: ornamental work made from gold or silver)
- o das Heptan (heptane)
- o das Hexan (hexane)
- o das Mangan (manganese)
- o das Marzipan[26] (marzipan/almond paste)
- o das Methan (methane)
- o das Nonan (nonane)
- o das Oktan (octane)
- o das Pentan (pentane gas)
- o das Porzellan (porcelain/ china/chinaware)
- o das Propan (propane)
- o das Titan (titanium)
- o das Tryptophan (tryptophan)
- o das Uran (uranium)
- o das Zellophan (cellophane)

Three other often-used neuter exceptions: *das LAN* (short for Local Area Network), *das WLAN* (short for Wireless Local Area Network), *das Organ* (body organ or institutional organ)

A very rare feminine exception to the *-an* ending: *die Membran* (membrane, same category as *die Haut*)

-ang:

- o der Anfang
- o der Drang
- o der Einklang
- o der Empfang
- o der Fang
- o der Gang
- o der Gesang[27]
- o der Hang
- o der Klang
- o der Mustang
- o der Rang

- o der Slang
- o der Strang (thread/cord/rope)
- o der Tang (seaweed)
- o der Vorhang

-ant:

Male persons or animals:

- o der Demonstrant
- o der Elefant
- o der Lieferant

Exceptions: inanimate objects or nouns imported from French, which would tend to make them neuter: *das Croissant, das Deodorant, das Restaurant*

-ast:

- o der Ballast (ballast)
- o der Bast (bast)
- o der Chloroplast (chloroplast)
- o der Damast (damask)
- o der Enthusiast (enthusiast)
- o der Fahnenmast (flagpole)
- o der Fantast/Phantast (dreamer/fantasist)
- o der Gast (guest)
- o der Gymnasiast (high-school pupil/student)
- o der Knast (prison)
- o der Kontrast (contrast)
- o der Mast[28] (mast)
- o der Morast (morass)
- o der Palast (palace)
- o der Seidelbast (daphne shrub)
- o der Toast[29] (toast)
- o der Zytoblast (cytoblast)

Feminine *-ast* exceptions (feminine tends to be the category of more abstract nouns):

- die Altlast (legacy)
- die Beweislast (burden of proof/onus)
- die Hast (haste)
- die Last (burden/load/weight)
- die Mast (fattening)
- die Rast (rest/respite)
- die Unrast (restlessness)

-auch:

- der Bauch
- der Brauch
- der Gebrauch (custom/practice/convention/use)
- der Knoblauch (garlic)
- der Lauch (leek)
- der Missbrauch
- der Rauch
- der Schlauch (hose)
- der Strauch (shrub)
- der Verbrauch

-aum:

- der Baum
- der Flaum (fluff/down)
- der Raum (space/area/room/scope)
- der Saum (hem/seam/edge)
- der Schaum (foam/froth)
- der Traum

-bold:

- der Kobold (goblin)
- der Lügenbold (inveterate liar)

o der Trunkenbold (drunkard)
o der Witzbold (joker)

-eg:

o der Abstieg
o der Ausstieg
o der Ausweg
o der Beleg
o der Krieg
o der Weg

Two exceptions of Latin origin, which would tend to make them neuter: das Privileg, das Sakrileg

-eis:

o der Ausweis
o der Kreis (same category as *der Ring, der Zirkel*)
o der Preis

-en: Around eighty per cent[30] of nouns ending on *-en* are masculine, with the remainder neuter. The *-en* ending is not typical for feminine nouns

o der Balken (the indicator bar/a beam of wood)
o der Ballen (bundle)
o der Barren (parallel bars/ingot)
o der Batzen (chunk/big portion)
o der Besen
o der Boden
o der Bogen
o der Braten
o der Brocken
o der Brunnen
o der Busen
o der Daumen

THE SECRETS OF GERMAN GENDER

- o der Degen
- o der Drachen
- o der Faden
- o der Felsen
- o der Fetzen (shred)
- o der Fladen
- o der Frieden
- o der Funken
- o der Galgen
- o der Garten
- o der Gaumen (palate)
- o der Glauben
- o der Graben
- o der Hafen
- o der Haken
- o der Haufen
- o der Hoden
- o der Hopfen
- o der Husten
- o der Karpfen (fish: carp, and fish tends to be masculine)
- o der Karren
- o der Kasten
- o der Klumpen
- o der Knochen
- o der Knoten
- o der Kolben (piston)
- o der Korken (cork or stopper)
- o der Kragen
- o der Krapfen
- o der Kuchen
- o der Laden
- o der Lappen
- o der Loden
- o der Magen
- o der Nacken
- o der Ofen
- o der Orden

o der Packen (heap/pile/stack)
o der Pfropfen
o der Rachen
o der Rahmen
o der Rasen
o der Rechen (rake)
o der Regen
o der Reifen
o der Rochen (fish: ray)
o der Roggen (rye)
o der Rücken
o der Samen
o der Schaden
o der Schinken
o der Schnupfen
o der Schuppen
o der Segen
o der Socken
o der Spaten
o der Stecken
o der Streifen
o der Tropfen
o der Wagen
o der Weizen
o der Zacken
o der Zapfen

Around twenty per cent of nouns ending on *-en* are neuter:[31]

- Nouns derived from verbs ending on *-en* are neuter:[32] das Essen, das Leben, das Wissen, das Schreiben, das Treffen, das Beben

- Diminutives ending on *-en* are neuter: das Küken, das Fohlen (newly-born horse/foal)

- Grammar/parts of speech tend to be a neuter category, hence also when the noun ends in *-en*: das Nomen

- Higher-level/first-order categories of classification tend to be neuter (see the chapter on neuter nouns for a more detailed explanation), which would then also be true for nouns in this category ending on *-en*: das Wesen, das Volumen, das Vermögen

- Several nouns associated with the bedroom (*das Schlafzimmer*) and the bathroom (*das Badezimmer*) tend to be neuter, and thus also for related nouns ending on *-en:* das Laken (sheet), das Kissen (pillow), das Leinen (linen), das Leintuch (bedsheet), das Bett (bed); das Becken (basin, sink/pond/pool), das Waschbecken (washing basin), das Bad (bath)

- Other neuter nouns ending on *-en:* das Examen (a French import, which would tend to make it neuter), das Eisen (iron – metals tend to be neuter), das Wappen (coat of arms/emblem/crest, in the same neuter category as *das Banner, das Hoheitszeichen*)

-ent: (but not typically *-ment*[33])

- o der Abiturient (a pupil/high-school student in their final year, or about to enter that year, or who has just graduated from that year)
- o der Abonnent (subscriber)
- o der Absolvent (graduate/alumnus/diploma holder)
- o der Advent
- o der Agent
- o der Akzent
- o der Assistent
- o der Barchent
- o der Cent

- o der Dirigent
- o der Dissident
- o der Dozent
- o der Exponent
- o der Gradient
- o der Koeffizient
- o der Konsument
- o der Kontinent
- o der Kontrahent
- o der Konvent
- o der Korrespondent
- o der Moment
- o der Okzident
- o der Opponent
- o der Orient
- o der Patient
- o der Präsident
- o der Produzent
- o der Quotient
- o der Referent
- o der Regent
- o der Resident
- o der Rezensent
- o der Student
- o der Zedent

Exceptions (neuter):

- o das Kontingent (from French/Latin origin)
- o das Patent (from the Latin, which would tend to make it neuter in German)
- o das Prozent (from the same category as fractions, which are typically neuter: das Viertel, etc.)
- o das Talent (originally a unit of weight, like *das Pfund,* which would make it neuter, but today refers to a natural aptitude or skill)
- o das Transparent (banner, hence also *das Banner*)

-er: Around seventy per cent of nouns ending on -er (but not on -ier)[34] are masculine.[35]

o der Acker (field/farmland/acre)
o der Anker (anchor)
o der Ärger
o der Bagger
o der Becher
o der Bedenkenträger (the doubter/naysayer)
o der Biber
o der Bohrer
o der Bunker
o der Donner
o der Dünger
o der Eifer
o der Eimer
o der Eiter
o der Fächer (fan for waving)
o der Falter (butterfly/moth)
o der Fehler
o der Filter
o der Finger
o der Fühler
o der Hafer
o der Hammer
o der Hamster
o der Höcker (camel's hump)
o der Hocker (stool/person who sits around too much)
o der Hummer
o der Hunger
o der Ingwer
o der Jammer
o der Kader (in Switzerland: *das* Kader)
o der Käfer
o der Kater
o der Keller

o der Kerker (dungeon)
o der Kleber
o der Köder (bait)
o der Koffer
o der Körper
o der Krater
o der Kühler
o der Kummer
o der Laser
o der Lüster (chandelier)
o der Ordner
o der Panzer
o der Sender
o der Sommer
o der Teller
o der Tiger
o der Walzer
o der Wecker
o der Winter
o der Zauber
o der Zeiger
o der Zucker

Nouns derived from verbs with the suffix –er tend to be masculine: arbeiten → *der Arbeiter*; fahren → *der Fahrer*; lehren → *der Lehrer*; spielen → *der Spieler*

Nouns, verbs or adjectives with -er, -ler, -ner, -iker added to them tend to be masculine: Eisenbahn → *der Eisenbahner*, Hamburg → *der Hamburger*, Sport → *der Sportler*, Rente → *der Rentner*, Alkohol → *der Alkoholiker*, fernsehen → *der Fernseher*, fehlen → *der Fehler*

Derivatives of numbers with an -er ending tend to be masculine: 50 → *der Fünfziger*

Exceptions: Around fifteen per cent of nouns ending on -er are feminine.[36]

One category of nouns ending on -er that is feminine are parts of the body:

- o die Ader (vein)
- o die Herzkammer (heart ventricle)
- o die Leber (liver)
- o die Schulter (shoulder)
- o die Wimper (eyelash)

Other feminine nouns ending on -er:

- o die Butter (used to have a feminine -a ending to it; also think of: die Kuh → die Milch → die Butter)[37]
- o die Dauer (duration; same category as *die Zeit*)
- o die Elster (magpie; smaller birds tend to be feminine)
- o die Faser (fibre: synonymous with *die Litze*, stranded wire)
- o die Feder (feather or a spring)
- o die Feier (celebration/ceremony/festival)
- o die Folter (torture: same feminine category as *die Quälerei, die Tortur*)
- o die Leiter (ladder; synonym of *die Verbindung*; derived from *die Leitung*)
- o die Marter (torture: the torment/ordeal)
- o die Mauer (synonym of *die Wand*; flat shapes tend to be feminine)
- o die Metapher (synonymous with *die Übertragung*)
- o die Oper (used to have an -a ending in the late 1700s)
- o die Steuer (tax; numbers are feminine)
- o die Trauer (grief; tears are feminine: *die Träne*)
- o die Ziffer (numbers are feminine)

Neuter exceptions: around fifteen per cent[38] of nouns ending on -er are neuter

- o das Alter (top-level category for age, usually measured in years, *das Jahr*)
- o das Banner (banner, imported from the French, and imported nouns tend to be neuter; alsó in the same neuter category as *das Hoheitszeichen, das Wappen*)
- o das Feuer (fire; some of the basic elements of nature tend to be neuter)
- o das Fieber (imported from Latin, which would tend to make it neuter)
- o das Futter (top-level category; food for animals)
- o das Gatter (gate; same category as *das Tor, das Portal, das Hindernis*)
- o das Gitter (iron railing/mesh; metals tend to be neuter)
- o das Kloster (from Latin for a residence for monks and nuns; same neuter category as *das Wohnhaus*)
- o das Kupfer (metals tend to be neuter)
- o das Lager (warehouse/storage/camp, same category as *das Vorratshaus, das Camp, das Depot*)
- o das Leder (leather: same animal produce category as fur, *das Fell*)
- o das Messer (metals and swords are neuter)
- o das Muster (same category as *das Beispiel*)
- o das Opfer (could refer to either an inanimate thing, such as an offering or sacrifice, or to a person: a male or a female victim)
- o das Pflaster (cobbled paving/plaster)
- o das Poster (imported nouns tend to be neuter)
- o das Pulver (powder)
- o das Ruder (helm/oar/rudder/wheel; same category as *das Steuer, das Paddel*)
- o das Silber (metals tend to be neuter)
- o das Ufer (same category as *das Land*)
- o das Wasser (water; the elements of nature tend to be neuter)

- das Wetter (same neuter category as *das Klima*)
- das Wunder (same neuter category as *das Geschehen, das Ereignis, das Staunen*)
- das Zimmer (room; originally from the verb *zimmern*, meaning to make something out of wood/timber (hence, *Zimmermann* = carpenter); in the same neuter category as *das Gemach* (chamber/room/abode), *das Haus, das Gebäude*)

-el: As in the case of *-er* endings (see above), *-el* endings also tend to be associated with masculine nouns. Around sixty per cent[39] of nouns ending on *-el* are masculine.

Masculine nouns ending on *-el*:

- der Apfel (which is an exception to the rule that fruit tends to be a feminine category)
- der Ärmel (sleeve)
- der Artikel
- der Beutel
- der Büffel
- der Bügel
- der Dackel (sausage dog; same category as *der Hund*)
- der Deckel (lid)
- der Egel (leech)
- der Engel
- der Esel
- der Flügel
- der Gipfel
- der Gürtel
- der Hagel
- der Handel
- der Hebel
- der Henkel
- der Himmel
- der Hügel
- der Igel (hedgehog)

- o der Jubel
- o der Kegel (skittle/geometric cone)
- o der Kessel (kettle/pot/cauldron)
- o der Kittel (professional jacket/coat/smock)
- o der Knöchel (ankle or knuckle)
- o der Knödel
- o der Knorpel (cartilage)
- o der Kübel
- o der Löffel (the spoon – an important household utensil that follows the -*el* gender tendency)
- o der Mangel
- o der Mantel
- o der Meissel (chisel)
- o der Mörtel (mortar: mixture of cement and sand)
- o der Muskel
- o der Nabel
- o der Nagel
- o der Nebel
- o der Pegel
- o der Pickel
- o der Pöbel (rabble/mob/riffraff)
- o der Pudel
- o der Rüssel (trunk, as in an elephant's trunk)
- o der Säbel (sabre)
- o der Schenkel
- o der Schlüssel
- o der Schnabel
- o der Sessel
- o der Sockel
- o der Stapel
- o der Tempel
- o der Titel
- o der Trubel (hustle and bustle)
- o der Tümpel (pond)
- o der Tunnel
- o der Vogel
- o der Winkel

- o der Wipfel (tree top)
- o der Würfel
- o der Zettel
- o der Ziegel (brick/tile)
- o der Zirkel
- o der Zweifel (doubt)

Exceptions: Around twenty-five per cent[40] of nouns ending on -el are feminine.

- birds (which tend to be feminine if they are not too large): die Amsel (blackbird), die Drossel (Thrush), die Wachtel (quail)

- the produce of plants tends to be feminine, hence also for some nouns ending on -el: die Dattel (date), die Distel (thistle), die Eichel (acorn), die Wurzel (root)

- just as in the case of nouns ending on -er, some parts of the body tend to be the exception to the masculine-ending -el tendency: die Achsel (armpit/underarm)

- some food and related utensils: die Muschel (seafood: clam, from the 9th century *muscula*), die Nudel, die Gabel (that important household utensil, the fork, is feminine – see the explanation in the Introduction), as are some other home instruments/utensils ending on -el: die Nadel, die Kordel (chord/string), die Kurbel (crank), die Tafel (a blackboard or a laid-out table, i.e. the top of the table)

- die Angel (hinge, fishing rod)

- phrases, rules and stories tend to be feminine: die Bibel, die Regel, die Klausel (clause/proviso/stipulation), die Fabel, die Floskel (an empty phrase; just saying something for the sake of saying it, but not really meaning it)

- objects shining/giving light: die Ampel (traffic light, like *die Lampe*), die Fackel (a burning torch, from the 8th century, *fackala*)

- die Insel (island, from the Latin *insula,* ending on the feminine *-a*)

- die Klientel (the client base, from the Latin *clientela,* ending on the feminine *-a*)

- die Kugel (which used to have a feminine *-e* ending to it in the Middle Ages), die Gondel (from the Italian *gondola,* with *-a* tending to be feminine), die Kapsel (from the Latin *capsula*), die Orgel (from the Latin *organa*), die Formel (from the Latin *formula*), die Geisel (hostage, male or female)

Exceptions: Around 15 per cent of nouns ending on *-el* are neuter.

- das Debakel (imported French word, which would tend to make it neuter; same category as *das Fiasko, das Desaster*)
- das Ferkel (piglet; diminutives tend to be neuter)
- das Hotel (same category as *das Gasthaus*; hotel names are neuter)
- das Kabel (same category as *das Seil*: rope/cable/cord)
- das Kapitel (part of *das Buch*; of Latin origin: *capitulum*, a neuter noun in Latin and neuter when imported into German)
- das Mittel (the means: linked to *das Geld, das Kapital*)
- das Nickel (metals tend to be neuter)
- das Orakel (can refer to a male or female person, or even to a thing; from the neuter Latin *oraculum*, which

would tend to make it neuter when imported into
German)
o das Paddel (imported word; same neuter category as *das
Ruder*)
o das Pendel (from the Latin *pendulum*)
o das Rätsel (same neuter category as *das Geheimnis, das
Mysterium; das Phänomen, das Wunder*)
o das Rudel (a pack/herd/swarm/horde: collectives tend to
be neuter, especially when they start with *Ge-*)
o das Segel (sail: from *das Tuchstück*)
o das Übel (evil: same neuter category as *das Böse, das
Leid*)
o das Wiesel (small animal: weasel)

-eur: (but not *-ur*)[41]

o der Akteur
o der Amateur
o der Charmeur
o der Chauffeur
o der Dekorateur
o der Deserteur
o der Dompteur
o der Dresseur
o der Exporteur
o der Filmregisseur
o der Flaneur
o der Friseur
o der Gouverneur
o der Graveur
o der Hasardeur
o der Importeur
o der Ingenieur
o der Innendekorateur
o der Inspekteur
o der Installateur
o der Instrukteur

- o der Jongleur
- o der Kollaborateur
- o der Kolporteur
- o der Kommandeur
- o der Konstrukteur
- o der Kontrolleur
- o der Marodeur
- o der Masseur
- o der Monteur
- o der Operateur
- o der Parfümeur
- o der Profiteur
- o der Provokateur
- o der Redakteur
- o der Regisseur
- o der Saboteur
- o der Schwadroneur
- o der Souffleur
- o der Spediteur
- o der Transporteur
- o der Voyeur

Exception: *das Interieur* (an inanimate thing, not a profession, role or activity).

-ich: Nouns ending on *-ich* are masculine 81 per cent of the time[42]

- o der Anstrich
- o der Ausgleich
- o der Bereich
- o der Deich (dike)
- o der Fittich (poetic: the wing of a bird; same category as *der Flügel*)
- o der Streich
- o der Strich
- o der Teich

- o der Teppich
- o der Vergleich
- o der Wüterich (someone who gets angry easily, goes berserk)

-ig: der Honig, der Käfig, der Teig, der Pfennig

-iker: (masculine 100 per cent of the time)

- o der Agnostiker
- o der Akademiker
- o der Alkoholiker
- o der Analytiker
- o der Aphoristiker
- o der Apokalyptiker
- o der Arithmetiker
- o der Asthmatiker
- o der Astrophysiker
- o der Automechaniker
- o der Bautechniker
- o der Biochemiker
- o der Botaniker
- o der Chemiker
- o der Computertechniker
- o der Diabetiker
- o der Dogmatiker
- o der Dramatiker
- o der Egozentriker
- o der Elektriker
- o der Elektroniker
- o der Elektrotechniker
- o der Epiker
- o der Epileptiker
- o der Esoteriker
- o der Ethiker
- o der Exzentriker
- o der Fanatiker

- o der Genetiker
- o der Grafiker/Graphiker
- o der Häretiker
- o der Heilpraktiker
- o der Historiker
- o der Hysteriker
- o der Informatiker
- o der Ironiker
- o der Keramiker
- o der Kernphysiker
- o der Klassiker
- o der Kleriker
- o der Komiker
- o der Kosmetiker
- o der Kritiker
- o der Kybernetiker
- o der Logiker
- o der Lyriker
- o der Marketingpraktiker
- o der Mathematiker
- o der Mechaniker
- o der Mimiker
- o der Musiker
- o der Mystiker
- o der Neurotiker
- o der Optiker
- o der Philharmoniker
- o der Physiker
- o der Polemiker
- o der Politiker
- o der Pragmatiker
- o der Praktiker
- o der Prognostiker
- o der Psychoanalytiker
- o der Psychotiker
- o der Rhetoriker
- o der Romantiker

- o der Sanguiniker
- o der Satiriker
- o der Skeptiker
- o der Statiker
- o der Statistiker
- o der Stoiker
- o der Taktiker
- o der Techniker
- o der Theoretiker
- o der Verschwörungstheoretiker
- o der Zahntechniker
- o der Zyniker

-ismus: (masculine 100 per cent of the time)

- o der Absolutismus
- o der Abstimmungsmechanismus
- o der Aktionismus
- o der Aktivismus
- o der Alkoholismus
- o der Alpinismus
- o der Altruismus
- o der Anachronismus
- o der Analphabetismus
- o der Anarchismus
- o der Anglizismus
- o der Antagonismus
- o der Antifaschismus
- o der Antikonformismus
- o der Antisemitismus
- o der Aphorismus
- o der Arabismus
- o der Archaismus
- o der Atavismus
- o der Atheismus
- o der Autismus
- o der Automatismus

- o der Behaviorismus
- o der Bilingualismus
- o der Bioterrorismus
- o der Buddhismus
- o der Calvinismus
- o der Chauvinismus
- o der Dadaismus
- o der Darwinismus
- o der Defätismus
- o der Deismus
- o der Despotismus
- o der Determinismus
- o der Dogmatismus
- o der Druckmechanismus
- o der Egalitarismus
- o der Egoismus
- o der Egozentrismus
- o der Elektromagnetismus
- o der Eskapismus
- o der Euphemismus
- o der Evolutionismus
- o der Exhibitionismus
- o der Existentialismus
- o der Exorzismus
- o der Expressionismus
- o der Extremismus
- o der Fanatismus
- o der Faschismus
- o der Fatalismus
- o der Feminismus
- o der Fetischismus
- o der Feudalismus
- o der Finanzkapitalismus
- o der Föderalismus
- o der Fundamentalismus
- o der Funktionalismus
- o der Futurismus

o der Germanismus
o der Gigantismus
o der Hedonismus
o der Hellenismus
o der Hinduismus
o der Humanismus
o der Idealismus
o der Imperialismus
o der Impressionismus
o der Individualismus
o der Intellektualismus
o der Internationalismus
o der Irrationalismus
o der Islamismus
o der Isolationismus
o der Journalismus
o der Judaismus
o der Kannibalismus
o der Kapitalismus
o der Katechismus
o der Katholizismus
o der Klassizismus
o der Kollektivismus
o der Kolonialismus
o der Kommunismus
o der Konformismus
o der Konfuzianismus
o der Konservatismus
o der Konsultationsmechanismus
o der Kreationismus
o der Kubismus
o der Kulturimperialismus
o der Laizismus
o der Leninismus
o der Liberalismus
o der Linksextremismus
o der Lobbyismus

- der Magnetismus
- der Maoismus
- der Marxismus
- der Masochismus
- der Massentourismus
- der Materialismus
- der Mechanismus
- der Metabolismus
- der Mikroorganismus
- der Militarismus
- der Minimalismus
- der Modernismus
- der Monotheismus
- der Moralismus
- der Multikulturalismus
- der Nationalismus
- der Nationalsozialismus
- der Naturalismus
- der Nazismus
- der Neoliberalismus
- der Neologismus
- der Neomarxismus
- der Nepotismus
- der Neuklassizismus
- der Nihilismus
- der Nonkonformismus
- der Nudismus
- der Ökotourismus
- der Opportunismus
- der Optimismus
- der Organismus
- der Paganismus
- der Parallelismus
- der Parlamentarismus
- der Paternalismus
- der Patriotismus
- der Pazifismus

- o der Perfektionismus
- o der Pessimismus
- o der Platonismus
- o der Pluralismus
- o der Populismus
- o der Pragmatismus
- o der Professionalismus
- o der Protektionismus
- o der Protestantismus
- o der Puritanismus
- o der Radikalismus
- o der Rassismus
- o der Rationalismus
- o der Realismus
- o der Rechtsextremismus
- o der Rechtsradikalismus
- o der Republikanismus
- o der Revanchismus
- o der Revisionismus
- o der Sadismus
- o der Schutzmechanismus
- o der Separatismus
- o der Sexismus
- o der Sicherungsmechanismus
- o der Skeptizismus
- o der Snobismus
- o der Sozialismus
- o der Subjektivismus
- o der Surrealismus
- o der Syllogismus
- o der Syndikalismus
- o der Terrorismus
- o der Thatcherismus
- o der Tourismus
- o der Tribalismus
- o der Utilitarismus
- o der Utopismus

- o der Vandalismus
- o der Veganismus
- o der Vegetarismus
- o der Voyeurismus
- o der Vulgarismus
- o der Zionismus
- o der Zündungsmechanismus
- o der Zynismus

Kn-:

- o der Knabe
- o der Knacker
- o der Knall
- o der Knebel
- o der Kniff
- o der Knopf
- o der Knüppel
- o der Knoblauch
- o der Knochen

(The more consonants at the beginning or end of the noun, the likelier that it is a masculine noun.[43] Exception: das Knie).

-ling: Nouns ending on *-ling,* but not necessarily on *-ing,*[44] tend to be masculine.

- o der Abkömmling (descendant/derivative/offspring/progeny)
- o der Ankömmling (newcomer)
- o der Dichterling (a bad poet)
- o der Drilling (person: triplet)
- o der Eindringling (intruder)
- o der Erdling (earthling)
- o der Flüchtling (refugee)
- o der Frühling (spring)
- o der Lehrling (student)

- der Liebling (favourite/darling)
- der Säugling (infant)
- der Schmetterling (butterfly)
- der Schützling (protégé)
- der Schwächling (wimp)
- der Zwilling (twin)

-mpf:

- der Dampf (steam/vapour)
- der Kampf
- der Krampf
- der Rumpf
- der Strumpf
- der Stumpf
- der Sumpf (swamp)
- der Trumpf

-ner: der Kenner (connoisseur), der Ordner (folder/file/dossier)

Exceptions: das Banner (imported foreign nouns tend to be neuter), die Wiener (when used as a reference to *die Wiener Wurst*)

-og:

- der Blog (also *das* Blog)
- der Dialog
- der Herzog
- der Katalog
- der Monolog
- der Smog
- der Sog (wake, as in "the wake left by the plane, ship or crisis")
- der Trog (trough/tray/vat)

-on: der Marathon, der Thron

-pf: Nouns that end with *-pf* are often masculine; der Kopf, der Zopf, der Napf, der Knopf, der Kropf, der Pfropf, der Schopf (a tuft of hair), der Topf, der Gugelhupf, der Unterschlupf (refuge/hideout)

Schwa-: der Schwabe, der Schwachsinn, der Schwall, der Schwamm, der Schwan, der Schwank, der Schwanz (Exceptions: die Schwalbe – the swallow, a bird, which also has the feminine *-e* ending)

-tel: see the entry above for *-el*

-u: ending on the unstressed *-u*

- o der Akku (abbreviation of *der Akkumulator*, battery)
- o der Bau
- o der Guru
- o der Klau
- o der Pneu (same masculine category as *der Reifen*)
- o der Stau
- o der Tofu
- o der Uhu (type of owl; larger birds tend to be masculine)

Nouns ending on the stressed *-u* tend not to be masculine (with the following examples all imported nouns, which would tend to make them neuter):

- o das Adieu
- o das Plateau
- o das Tabu
- o das Tiramisu

-uch: Nouns ending on *-uch* are masculine or neuter.

- o der Abbruch
- o der Besuch

- o der Bruch
- o der Einbruch
- o der Einspruch
- o der Eunuch
- o der Fluch
- o der Geruch/der Ruch
- o der Spruch
- o der Umbruch
- o der Unterbruch
- o der Versuch
- o der Zuspruch

Neuter examples:

- o das Buch
- o das Gesuch (written application/petition/plea; documents tend to be neuter: *das Schreiben, das Wort, das Papier, das Blatt, das Dokument, das Buch*)
- o das Tuch

-ug: der Flug, der Abflug, der Ausflug, der Zug, der Anzug, der Einzug, der Umzug, der Unfug

-und: der Bund, der Grund, der Schund (trash/filth), der Hund, der Fund, der Schwund (decrease/decline/dwindling), der Schlund (pharynx), der Mund (Exception, neuter: das Pfund)

-us:

- o der Abakus
- o der Airbus
- o der Bonus
- o der Bus
- o der Campus
- o der Diskus
- o der Exodus
- o der Fiskus

- o der Fokus
- o der Kaktus
- o der Malus
- o der Modus
- o der Nexus
- o der Radius
- o der Status
- o der Tetanus
- o der Typhus
- o der Typus
- o der Zirkus
- o der Zyklus

Exceptions, neuter:

- o das Genus (grammatical gender)
- o das Haus
- o das Minus
- o das Opus
- o das Plus
- o das Virus (in technical, scientific use the preference is for *das Virus*, but in colloquial language *der* is also sometimes used)

Exceptions, feminine:

- o die Maus (smaller animals not ending on *-er* tend to be feminine)
- o die Venus (both the Roman goddess of love as well as the planet)

Sounds also relate to how long or short words are. Studies have shown that short, one-syllable nouns tend to be overwhelmingly masculine, followed by neuter and feminine.[45]

One-syllable nouns that are masculine (notice the frequency of consonants at the beginning and end of the nouns):

- o der Arm
- o der Darm
- o der Gott
- o der Spott
- o der Schrott
- o der Fuss
- o der Fluss
- o der Guss
- o der Kuss
- o der Schluss
- o der Schuss
- o der Schein
- o der Stein
- o der Wein
- o der Brei
- o der Schrei
- o der Klatsch
- o der Tratsch
- o der Druck
- o der Ruck
- o der Schluck
- o der Schmuck
- o der Schwanz
- o der Kranz
- o der Zins
- o der Mix
- o der Tee
- o der Chip
- o der Clip
- o der Trip

Single-syllable nouns starting with *Kn-* tend to be masculine (especially if they end on a consonant):

- o der Knack
- o der Knall
- o der Knast
- o der Knauf
- o der Knecht
- o der Knick
- o der Kniff
- o der Knopf

(Exception: das Knie)

Single-syllable nouns ending with *-t* tend to be masculine:

- der Staat

from which follow many compound nouns:

- o der Agrarstaat
- o der Bundesstaat
- o der Dienstleistungsstaat
- o der Einheitsstaat
- o der Feudalstaat
- o der Golfstaat
- o der Industriestaat
- o der Inselstaat
- o der Kirchenstaat
- o der Kleinstaat
- o der Küstenstaat
- o der Mitgliedsstaat
- o der Nachbarstaat
- o der Nationalstaat
- o der Ölstaat
- o der Oststaat
- o der Polizeistaat

- o der Rechtsstaat
- o der Satellitenstaat
- o der Schurkenstaat
- o der Sozialstaat
- o der Stadtstaat
- o der Vasallenstaat
- o der Wohlfahrtsstaat

- der Markt

from which follow many frequently-used compound nouns:

- o der Agrarmarkt
- o der Aktienmarkt
- o der Binnenmarkt
- o der Devisenmarkt
- o der Kreditmarkt

- der Saft

from which follow all the types of juice imaginable:

der Apfelsaft, der Fruchtsaft, der Hustensaft, der Orangensaft, der Tomatensaft, der Traubensaft, der Zitronensaft

- der Wert

from which follow a huge number of compound nouns, especially used in technical language when things are measured:

- o der Anfangswert
- o der Anlagewert
- o der Anpassungswert
- o der Bauwert
- o der Bodenwert
- o der Bruttowert
- o der Buchungswert

- o der Buchwert
- o der Defaultwert
- o der Depotwert
- o der Dezimalwert
- o der Durchschnittswert
- o der Emissionswert
- o der Endwert
- o der Erfahrungswert
- o der Ertragswert
- o der Extremwert
- o der Gegenwert
- o der Geldwert
- o der Gesamtwert
- o der Grenzwert
- o der Grundwert
- o der Handelswert
- o der Höchstwert
- o der Indexwert
- o der Kalorienwert
- o der Kapitalwert
- o der Kaufwert
- o der Kennwert
- o der Kurswert
- o der Marktwert
- o der Maximalwert
- o der Mehrwert
- o der Mietwert
- o der Mindestwert
- o der Mittelwert
- o der Nettowert
- o der Nominalwert
- o der Realwert
- o der Restwert
- o der Seltenheitswert
- o der Sollwert
- o der Standardwert
- o der Toleranzwert

- o der Umrechnungswert
- o der Wiederverkaufswert

- der Test (from which follows many compound nouns: e.g. der Abgastest, der Backtest, der Dopingtest)

- der Draht (wire, from which follows compound nouns like *der Stacheldraht*, barbed wire)

- der Bart, der Start, der Wart (person responsible for something, from which *der Abwart*), but *die* Gegenwart, because it is the synonym of *die Jetztzeit, die Präsenz*

- der Hut

- Single-syllable nouns ending with -*d* tend to be masculine:

der Brand, der Bund, der Feind, der Fjord, der Fund, der Held, der Herd, der Fond, der Grad, der Hund, der Mond, der Mund, der Neid, der Pfad, der Rand, der Sand, der Stand, der Sold, der Tod, der Trend, der Wind

The neuter and feminine exceptions can usually be explained by Rule 1 (categories).

- o Neuter, single-syllable nouns ending on -*d*: das Bad, das Bild, das Glied, das Kleid, das Gold (metals tend to be neuter), das Hemd, das Jod (chemical substances tend to be neuter), das Kind, das Land, das Leid, das Lied, das Rad, das Pferd, das Rind, das Pfund (units of weight tend to be neuter), das Feld, das Wild

- o Other one-syllable nouns that are neuter: das Bein (leg), das Blut (blood), das Buch, das Feld, das Floss, das Gut (as in das Kulturgut), das Haar (hair), das Heim, das Herz (heart), das Ja, das Nein, das Jein (an answer between yes

and no), das Kinn (chin), das Knie (knee), das Ohr (ear),
das Ross, das Schloss, das Sein, das Tuch, das Zelt

o Feminine, single-syllable nouns ending on -*d*: die Hand,
die Jagd (the feminine origin of hunting is explained in the
Introduction), die Magd, die Wand (flat shapes tend to be
feminine)

o Other one-syllable nouns that are feminine: die Kur, die
Uhr, die Nuss

- Nouns without a suffix derived from verbs tend to be
masculine:

o fallen → der Fall
o fangen → der Fang
o fluchen → der Fluch
o gehen → der Gang
o hängen → der Hang
o klingen → der Klang
o küssen → der Kuss
o sprechen → der Spruch
o zwingen → der Zwang

Sometimes also neuter: spielen → das Spiel; zelten → das Zelt;
and less frequently, feminine: fliehen → die Flucht; wählen →
die Wahl

-x:

Masculine: der Index, der Aktienindex, der DAX (Deutscher
Aktienindex), der Bordeaux, der Komplex, der Kodex, der
Reflex, der Sex

Feminine: die Box (while imported from English, which should
tend to make it neuter, *Box* is feminine, because it is in the same

feminine category as *die Büchse,* a container); die Mailbox, die Crux, die Matrix

Neuter: das Paradox (imported from Greek, which would tend to make it neuter), das Präfix, das Suffix (grammatical terms tend to be neuter)

Die: The rules that make nouns feminine

Rule 1: Categories

Numbers and mathematics: die Nummer, die Ziffer, die Zahl, die Null, die Eins, die Drei, die Algebra, die Mathematik, die Geometrie, die Rechnung, die Steuer (tax)

Time, especially the shortest time-spans: die Zeit, die Uhr, die Stunde, die Minute, die Sekunde; the longest time-periods are neuter: das Jahr, das Jahrzehnt (decade), das Jahrhundert (century), das Jahrtausend (millenium), and the periods in-between are masculine: der Tag, der Monat. The exceptions occur when the noun ends on the feminine *-e*: die Woche, die Dekade, die Epoche

Authority, power and governance: die Kraft (force/effect/ strength), die Macht (power/might/strength), die Power, die Leistung, die Energie, die Stärke, die Festigkeit, die Belastbarkeit, die Gewalt (force/violence), die Befugnis (authorization), die Wucht (impact/force/momentum), die Potenz, die Mächtigkeit, die Herrschaft (rule/domination/ dominion), die Vollmacht (power of attorney), die Behörde, die Autorität, die Regierung, die Kontrolle (monitoring/control/ supervision), die Steuerung (management/governance), die Steuer (tax), die Zahlung (payment/settlement)

Rules, permission and limits: die Regelung (regulation/ provision/arrangement/settlement), die Justiz, die Erlaubnis, die Frist, die Limitierung, die Grenze, die Begrenzung, die Beschränkung

Knowledge and wisdom: Wisdom is a feminine noun in both Greek and Latin, and is treated as a feminine concept in English in the Bible: "Yet wisdom is justified by *her* deeds." (Matthew 11:19). Perhaps not too surprisingly, therefore, knowledge and wisdom are feminine in German too: die Art, die Besonnenheit, die Bildung, die Einsicht, die Gerechtigkeit, die Intelligenz, die Justiz, die Kenntnis, die Klugheit, die Kunst, die Methode, die Methodik, die Philosophie, die Ratio, die Sorgfalt, die Technik, die Technologie, die Umsicht, die Vorausschau, die Voraussicht, die Vorsicht, die Vernunft, die Weise, die Weisheit, die Weitsicht

Communication: die Kommunikation, die Rede, die Frage, die Antwort,[46] die Replik, die Sprache, die Prosa, die Dichtung, die Sprachform, die Literatur, die Vorstellung, die Präsentation, die Metapher, die Übertragung, die Wiedergabe, die Erwiderung, die Entgegnung, die Besprechung, die Kritik, die Rezension, die Darstellung, die Moderation, die Vorführung, die Fabel, die Floskel (an empty phrase/just saying something for the sake of saying it, but not really meaning it). Exceptions can be explained by Rule 2. Nouns starting with *Ge-* tend to be neuter, hence, *das Gespräch, das Gerede*; nouns ending with *-og* tend to be masculine, hence, *der Dialog*.

Musical instruments: die Musik, die Orgel, die Flöte, die Harfe, die Mundharmonika, die Geige, die Violine, die Konzertina, die Gitarre, die Glocke, die Mandoline, die Oboe, die Trompete (for exceptions, please see endnote 47)

Form and shape:[48] die Form, die Gestalt (form/shape/figure), die Figur, die Silhouette, die Gestaltung (design/layout/composition)

- **Flat shapes:**

  o die Ablage (tray/shelf/rack)
  o die Bildfläche (screen/picture surface)

- o die Bohle (plank)
- o die Bramme (slab)
- o die Decke (ceiling)
- o die Ebene (level/plane/tier/plain)
- o die Fläche (area/surface/plane)
- o die Flanke (edge/flank/side)
- o die Fliese (slab/tile)
- o die Kulisse (backdrop)
- o die Platte (tile/plate/panel/board/slab/ledge)
- o die Schale (tray)
- o die Scheibe (slice)
- o die Schublade (drawer)
- o die Seite
- o die Tafel (blackboard)
- o die Theke (counter/bar counter)
- o die Tischplatte (table top/ table surface)
- o die Tragfläche (aircraft wing)
- o die Tür
- o die Wand (wall/side), die Mauer (wall)

- **Sharp shapes:**

  - o die Brosche (brooch/pin)
  - o die Forke (pitchfork)
  - o die Gabel (fork)
  - o die Klinge, die Schneide (blade/cutting edge)
  - o die Lanze (lance/spear)
  - o die Nadel (needle)
  - o die Schraube (screw)
  - o die Spitze (top/apex/nib/point/sharp-edge/peak)
  - o die Spritze (syringe)
  - o die Zinke (prong/tooth/tine/sharp point)

- **Pincer shapes:**

  - o die Klaue (claw)
  - o die Kralle (talon)

- o die Pratze (fork hook)
- o die Schere (scissors)
- o die Zange (pliers/tongs/pincer)

- **Hollow shapes:**

- o die Box
- o die Büchse (box/can)
- o die Dose (can/tin)
- o die Flasche
- o die Grotte
- o die Höhle (cave)
- o die Hülle (shell/case)
- o die Kiste (crate/chest)
- o die Röhre
- o die Schachtel (box)
- o die Schlucht (gorge/canyon/ravine)
- o die Schüssel (bowl)
- o die Trommel (drum/cylinder/barrel)
- o die Tube

Most rivers in central Europe: die Aare, die Limmat, die Reuss, die Rhone, die Donau, die Mosel, die Elbe, die Weser, die Oder (Exceptions: der Rhein, der Main) and rivers outside Europe ending on -a or -e

Hunting: This has to be feminine because the Greeks and Romans each had a goddess of hunting, Artemis and Diana: die Jagd, die Suche, die Verfolgung, die Hetze, die Flucht, die Wildnis

Food and sustenance: die Nahrung (food/nutrition/diet/ nourishment), die Speise (food/dish/meal), die Kost; the food provided by female mammals: die Milch, die Muttermilch (breast milk)

Gestures: die Geste (gesture), die Gestik, die Gebärde, die Bewegung, die Attitüde, die Körperhaltung, die Körpersprache, die Haltung, die Positur, die Stellung, die Pose

Seafaring signals, the navy and sailing craft: die Bake (beacon), die Boje (buoy), die Tonne (buoy), die Marine (the navy), die Handelsmarine, die Kriegsmarine, die Flotte, die Navy, die Jacht/die Yacht

Temperature: die Temperatur

- o Heat and hot places: die Sonne, die Glut (ember/glow/heat), die Wärme, die Hitze, die Wüste, die Sahara, die Hölle, die Heizung, die Wärmesenke (heat sink)

- o Cold and cold places: die Kälte, die Frostigkeit, die Erkältung, die Arktis, die Antarktis, die Kühle

Motorcycle brands: die BMW (only the motorcycle, not the car), die Yamaha

Types of planes: die Boeing 747, die Challenger, die Tupolew; but *der Airbus* because of *der Bus*

Names of ships: (even in cases where the noun would otherwise be masculine) die Bismarck, die Titanic, and even though the overall category is neuter (das Schiff, das Boot)

Animals with the feminine noun endings -e (die Schildkröte, die Giraffe, but not always) or -in (die Löwin), or domesticated providers of milk (die Kuh, die Geiss, die Ziege) or eggs (die Gans, die Henne) or smaller animals not ending on -er (e.g. die Maus) are usually feminine

Several types of bird are feminine: (especially smaller ones) die Amsel (blackbird), die Drossel (thrush), die Ente (duck), die

Elster (magpie; a rare example of an -*er* ending for a feminine noun because early versions of the noun ended on a feminine -*a*), die Eule (owl), die Gans (goose), die Krähe (crow), die Möwe (gull), die Nachtigall (nightingale), die Schwalbe (swallow), die Taube (dove), die Wachtel (quail). The masculine exceptions of birds ending on a vowel associated with feminine nouns are rare: der Falke (hawk), der Papagei (parrot).

Many insects are feminine: (especially if they end on the feminine -*e*) die Ameise, die Biene, die Fliege, die Grille, die Libelle, die Mücke, die Spinne, die Wespe, die Zecke, die Zikade; there is also a large group of insects that have endings associated with masculine nouns, e.g. der Floh, der Käfer

A lot of trees are feminine: die Buche (beech), die Eiche (oak), die Birke, die Kiefer, die Palme, die Pappel (poplar), die Tanne. Some exceptions: der Ahorn (maple tree), der Wacholder (juniper tree)

Flowers: (especially if they end on the feminine -*e*) die Rose, die Tulpe, die Nelke (carnation), die Mimose, die Chrysantheme, with several exceptions, especially if they end on -*en* used for diminutives, which is associated with neuter nouns: das Stiefmütterchen (pansy), das Veilchen (violet)

Fruit: die Ananas, die Apfelsine, die Aprikose, die Banane, die Birne, die Erdbeere, die Dattel, die Feige, die Guave, die Grapefruit, die Kiwi, die Kirsche, die Kokosnuss, die Kumquat, die Litschi, die Mandel, die Mango, die Melone, die Nuss, die Orange, die Pflaume, die Quitte, die Zitrone (exceptions: der Apfel, der Granatapfel, der Pfirsich – the latter three follow the *sounds* rule: nouns ending on -*el* are overwhelmingly masculine; and nouns ending and starting with lots of consonants tend to be masculine, as *Pfirsich* deserves to be)

Toothpaste and toothpaste brands: die Zahnpasta, die Colgate

Typeface: die Helvetica

Software: die Software (synonym of *die Programm-ausstattung*), die Malware, die Ransomware (*die Erpressersoftware*), die Applikation (which can give you the abbreviation *die App*, or if you think the word App refers to *das Programm*, then you can ascribe a neuter gender to it – both genders are accepted for *App*)

Nouns denoting female persons and functions are usually feminine: die Mutter, die Tochter, die Frau, die Schwester, but not always. Exceptions: das Mädchen (because of Rule 2: diminutives are neuter). To change a designation to explicitly feminine, one typically uses the ending *-in*: die Lehrerin, die Kaiserin, die Königin, die Ärztin.

Rule 2: Sounds

In German, as in Greek and Latin, words ending on *-a* and *-e* have a higher probability of being feminine.

-a: Nouns ending on *-a* tend to be feminine, especially if their roots are in Greek or Latin nouns that end in *-a*, but this is not always the case (see below): die Ära, die Agenda, die Algebra, die Angina, die Aorta, die Arena, die Aula, die Diva, die Fauna, die Flora, die Gala, die Kamera, die Lava, die Lira, die Mama, die Malaria, die Pasta, die Paella, die Peseta, die Pizza, die Quinoa, die Sauna, die Siesta, die Villa, die Viola

Exceptions: Nouns of Greek origin ending on *-ma*

- o das Aroma
- o das Asthma
- o das Charisma

- o das Dilemma
- o das Dogma
- o das Drama
- o das Klima
- o das Komma
- o das Magma
- o das Plasma
- o das Schema
- o das Schisma
- o das Sperma
- o das Stigma
- o das Thema
- o das Trauma

But *die Firma* (because it is not of Greek origin and is a synonym of *die Gesellschaft*)

-acht: die Acht, die Fracht, die Macht, die Pracht, die Jacht/Yacht, die Pacht, die Tracht, die Wacht (keeping watch), die Zwietracht (discord), die Eintracht (harmony); but *der* Verdacht (suspicion)

-ade: die Arkade, die Akkolade, die Ballade, die Barrikade, die Brigade, die Blockade, die Marmelade, die Fassade, die Dekade, die Eskapade, die Parade, die Gnade, die Gerade, die Kaskade, die Schublade, die Limonade, die Marinade, die Passage, die Schokolade, die Olympiade, die Promenade, die Roulade, die Serenade, die Tirade

-age: die Garage, die Montage, die Etage, die Spionage, die Persiflage, die Blamage

-anz: die Bausubstanz, die Bilanz, die Brillanz, die Diskrepanz, die Dominanz, die Eleganz, die Instanz, die Toleranz (but *der Kranz* because one-syllable nouns tend to be masculine)

-art: Some nouns derived from *die Art*: die Eigenart, die Gangart, die Sportart, die Tonart

-e: Nouns ending on *-e* are feminine around 90 per cent of the time.[49] Nouns ending on *-e* are usually feminine if they do not mean a male person (e.g. der Junge) and do not begin with the unstressed syllable *Ge-* (e.g. der Gedanke). Further exceptions are discussed below. Nouns with a derived suffix *-e* are always feminine: reden → die Rede, flach → die Fläche. Also, note that the addition of an *-e* at the end of the noun means that it is pronounced, which automatically means that even short words ending on an *-e* must have more than one syllable. This would help to explain why one-syllable words are less likely to be feminine; statistically, they are more likely to be masculine.

Examples of feminine nouns ending on *-e*:

die Adresse, die Ameise, die Analyse, die Banane, die Beute, die Biene, die Bitte, die Blume, die Bremse, die Brücke, die Decke, die Diagnose, die Ebbe, die Ecke, die Ehe, die Erde, die Fahne, die Falle, die Farbe, die Flagge, die Fliege, die Flöte, die Frage, die Freude, die Gasse, die Giraffe, die Gitarre, die Grenze, die Hose, die Jacke, die Kanne, die Kante, die Kappe, die Karte, die Kirsche, die Klasse, die Kleie (bran), die Krabbe, die Kreide, die Krise, die Krücke, die Lampe, die Liebe, die Lippe, die Liste, die Lücke, die Lüge, die Lunge, die Masse, die Matte, die Melone, die Messe, die Minute, die Motte, die Narbe, die Nase, die Nonne, die Oase, die Oboe, die Pause, die Pfanne, die Pflanze, die Pflaume, die Presse, die Rasse, die Ratte, die Reise, die Rolle, die Sache, die Schlange, die Schnecke, die Schokolade, die Schule, die Seele, die Seite, die Sekunde, die Socke, die Sonne, die Sorge, die Spange, die Speise, die Spinne, die Sprache, die Strasse, die Strecke, die Stunde, die Suche, die Summe, die Suppe, die Taille (waistline), die Tanne, die Tasse, die Toilette, die Tomate, die Tonne, die Treue, die Trompete, die Vase, die Violine, die Waffe, die Wange, die Wespe, die

Wiese, die Wonne (bliss), die Zange, die Zecke, die Zelle, die Zinswende, die Zunge

Exceptions: Just under ten per cent of the nouns ending on -e are masculine.[50] Since an -e ending is statistically not typically masculine, some such nouns are called "weak nouns" ("schwache Nomen"). An alternative name for some of this group is "die N-Deklination" because they typically add an extra "n" in the accusative, dative and genitive singular.

Examples of masculine nouns ending on -e:

o der Buchstabe
o der Friede
o der Funke
o der Gedanke
o der Junge
o der Name
o der Same
o der Wille

Some nationalities ending on -e are masculine:

der Afghane, der Baske, der Brite, der Bulgare, der Chinese, der Däne, der Franzose, der Grieche, der Ire, der Kroate, der Kurde, der Mongole, der Pole, der Russe, der Schotte, der Türke

Some nouns describing persons/functions that end in -e are masculine:

o der Angsthase
o der Bote
o der Bube
o der Bursche
o der Erbe (heir; the inheritance = *das Erbe*)
o der Experte
o der Gatte

- der Gefährte (companion)
- der Heide
- der Insasse
- der Junge
- der Junggeselle
- der Knabe
- der Kollege
- der Kommilitone (fellow student/classmate)
- der Komplize
- der Kunde
- der Laie
- der Neffe
- der Riese
- der Sklave
- der Zeuge

Some nouns for animals ending on -*e* are masculine:

- der Affe
- der Bulle
- der Drache
- der Hase
- der Falke
- der Löwe
- der Ochse
- der Rabe
- der Schimpanse
- der Welpe (pup/cub – an unusual exception to the rule that diminutives tend to be neuter)

Some professions ending on -*e* are masculine:

der Biologe, der Gynäkologe, der Pädagoge, der Soziologe, der Stratege (strategist)

A frequently-used noun ending on -*e* that is masculine is *der Käse*. This comes from the Latin word for cheese, *caseus*, which is masculine, and was imported into German after they already had a masculine noun for soft cheese, *der Quark*.

Less than one per cent of the nouns ending on *-e* are neuter:[51]

o das Auge
o das Ende
o das Erbe (inheritance, legacy; the person inheriting = *der Erbe*)
o das Finale (Italian)
o das Genre (imported French word, which would tend to be neuter)
o das Image (French)
o das Interesse (of Latin origin, which would tend to make it neuter)
o das Karate (types of sport tend to be neuter)
o das Konklave (of Latin origin, which would tend to make it neuter; this noun is also in the same neuter category as *das Gemach*, a room, chamber or abode)
o das Prestige (French)
o das Prozedere (Italian)
o das Regime (French)

Nous ending on *-e*, but which start with *Ge-* (which would tend to make them neuter):

o das Gebäude
o das Gebirge
o das Gefrage
o das Gemälde

Nouns derived from adjectives, which would make them neuter: das Gute, das Böse

-ee:

o die Allee (synonym of *die Strasse*)

- o die Armee (synonym of *die Wehrmacht, die Wehr, die Bundeswehr, die Abwehr*, from which follows also *die Feuerwehr*)
- o die Fee
- o die Idee
- o die Matinee
- o die Moschee
- o die Odyssee
- o die Orchidee
- o die Soiree
- o die Tournee

And then there is the important noun *die See* (sea), which becomes a lake when used with the masculine article because inland waters, like rivers, dams and canals, are masculine: *der See*. This variability around what to call large expanses of water is also found in English, where a lake can also be referred to as a sea, as in "the Sea of Galilee". Hence, German has several words for sea, each with a different gender: *die See* (sea), *das Meer* and *der Ozean* (ocean: the really big sea between continents). The sea is powerful enough, therefore, to violate Rule 1: categories of similar things tend to have a similar gender.

Exceptions in neuter (usually imported words, which would tend to make them neuter):

- o das Exposee/Exposé
- o das Frisbee
- o das Komitee
- o das Kanapee/ Canapé
- o das Püree
- o das Klischee
- o das Kommunikee/Kommuniqué
- o das Negligee/Negligé
- o das Renommee
- o das Resümee

o das Soufflee/Soufflé

-ei/-erei: If the noun has been formed from another noun or verb by adding *-erei*, then it is always feminine.

o die Angeberei (bravado)
o die Aufschneiderei (boasting)
o die Augenwischerei (to engage in a sham/to pretend)
o die Bäckerei (bakery)
o die Bauernfängerei (con game)
o die Beisserei (fighting involving teeth)
o die Bergsteigerei (mountain climbing)
o die Betrügerei (fraud/scam)
o die Bildhauerei (sculpture)
o die Brandmalerei (pyrography)
o die Brauerei (brewery)
o die Brennerei (distillery)
o die Bücherei (bookstore)
o die Druckerei (printing plant)
o die Duzerei (the act of referring to people in the informal *Du*, instead of by the more formal *Sie*)
o die Effekthascherei (cheap showmanship)
o die Faulenzerei (loafing around)
o die Feinbäckerei (confectionary)
o die Fischerei (fishing industry or fishing)
o die Fleischerei (meat market)
o die Flickerei (patching)
o die Fliegerei (aviation/flying)
o die Flunkerei (fibbing/telling stories)
o die Försterei (place where a forest ranger lives or works)
o die Freibeuterei (piracy)
o die Freimaurerei (Freemasonary)
o die Gaunerei (swindle)
o die Geheimniskrämerei (secretiveness)
o die Geheimnistuerei (culture of secrecy)
o die Geheimtuerei (collusion, typically done in secret)
o die Gerberei (tannery)

- o die Giesserei (foundry)
- o die Gleichmacherei (levelling down/making things equal)
- o die Haarspalterei (hair-splitting)
- o die Hehlerei (receiving stolen goods)
- o die Heimlichtuerei (being secretive)
- o die Hellseherei (clairvoyance)
- o die Hexerei (witchcraft)
- o die Imkerei (beekeeping)
- o die Jägerei (hunting)
- o die Kaffeerösterei (coffee roasting house)
- o die Käserei (cheese factory)
- o die Kellerei (wine producer)
- o die Ketzerei (heresy)
- o die Kinderei (childishness)
- o die Klempnerei (plumbing)
- o die Kletterei (climbing)
- o die Knallerei (ongoing loud noise)
- o die Küsserei (constant kissing)
- o die Landstreicherei (vagrancy)
- o die Lautmalerei (onomatopoeia)
- o die Leichenfledderei (robbing dead people)
- o die Liebedienerei (submissive or sychophantic behaviour)
- o die Liebhaberei (hobby)
- o die Lügerei (constant lying)
- o die Malerei (painting)
- o die Massenschlägerei (mass brawl/free-for-all fighting)
- o die Metzgerei (butchery)
- o die Meuterei (mutiny)
- o die Molkerei (where farmers bring the milk)
- o die Rechthaberei (always wanting to be right/bossiness)
- o die Reederei (shipping company)
- o die Schlamperei (sloppiness)
- o die Schlemmerei (gluttony)
- o die Schönfärberei (pretending that things are better than they are)
- o die Schreinerei (carpenter's workshop)
- o die Schufterei (drudgery)

- o die Schurkerei (villainous behaviour)
- o die Schwarzmalerei (always seeing the glass half empty)
- o die Schweinerei (underhandedness/mess)
- o die Seeräuberei (sea piracy)
- o die Sklaverei (slavery)
- o die Vereinsmeierei (exaggerated sense of importance by being a member of one or more clubs)
- o die Vielweiberei (polygamy)
- o die Völlerei (gluttony)
- o die Waffenmeisterei (armoury)
- o die Wahrsagerei (fortune telling)
- o die Weberei (weaving plant)
- o die Wichtigtuerei (pretending to be important)
- o die Wilddieberei (poaching)
- o die Wortklauberei (quibbling)
- o die Zahlenspielerei (to play games with numbers)
- o die Zauberei (magic)
- o die Zuhälterei (pimping)
- o die Zuträgerei (inform on someone, gossip)

Feminine nouns ending on *-ei*, but not on *-erei*: die Abtei, die Anwaltskanzlei, die Arznei, die Bastelei, die Bettelei, die Bummelei, die Bundeskriminalpolizei, die Bundespartei, die Detektei, die Polizei, die Kanzlei, die Partei

Exceptions, neuter nouns ending on *-ei*: das Ei, das Geschrei (starts with *Ge-*, which tends to be neuter)

Exceptions, masculine nouns ending on *-ei*: der Papagei (larger birds tend to be masculine), der Schrei (a one-syllable noun that is the synonym of *der Ruf, der Hilferuf*)

-enz: die Intelligenz, die Konsequenz, die Existenz, die Tendenz, die Frequenz

-falt: die Vielfalt, die Sorgfalt

-grafie/graphie: die Biografie, die Orthografie

-heit: die Dummheit, die Freiheit, die Gesundheit, die Sicherheit, die Wahrheit (but *das Fahrenheit*, because units measuring temperature tend to be neuter)[52]

-icht: (given that *Sicht* is feminine, there are several feminine nouns with this root; note how they coincide with the feminine category of "wisdom and knowledge")

- o die Sicht (view/point of view/perspective)
- o die Absicht (intention)
- o die Ansicht (view/opinion)
- o die Aufsicht (supervision)
- o die Aussicht (prospect/view)
- o die Einsicht (insight/access)
- o die Hinsicht (respect/regard)
- o die Nachsicht (forbearance)
- o die Übersicht (overview)
- o die Umsicht (prudence/caution/thoughtfulness)
- o die Vorsicht (caution)

In this category of feminine nouns, we also find *die Gicht* (gout), *die Nachricht, die Pflicht, die Schicht* (layer/shift/class).

Given that nouns beginning with *Ge-* tend to be neuter, we have:

- o das Gedicht
- o das Gericht
- o das Gesicht
- o das Gewicht

Other neuter nouns with this ending include *das Licht*, and its many derivatives, including *das Zwielicht* (twilight).

Masculine nouns ending on *-icht* include:

- o der Bericht (report, which is related to *der Unterricht* (teaching/instruction/education, which used to be a more masculine thing)
- o der Bösewicht (villain)
- o der Habicht (hawk)
- o der Verzicht (waiver/renunciation)
- o der Wicht (goblin/scoundrel)

-ie: (nouns ending on *-ie* are feminine 95 per cent of the time)[53] die Biologie, die Demokratie, die Diplomatie, die Familie, die Magie, die Melodie, die Monotonie, die Philosophie, die Psychologie, die Studie

Exceptions (masculine nouns ending on *-ie* typically relate to persons): der Hippie, der Junkie

Exceptions (neuter nouns ending on *-ie* typically relate to inanimate objects or to words starting with *Ge-*): das Knie, das Genie, das Selfie

-ik: die Musik, die Politik, die Physik, die Klassik, die Gotik, die Romantik, die Kritik, die Logik, die Ethik, die Symbolik, die Mechanik (neuter exception: *das Mosaik*, same category as *das Bild*)

-in: die Doktrin (doctrine); and professions and roles with the feminine form *-in* added, e.g. die Ärztin, die Studentin

Exceptions (masculine nouns ending on *-in*):

- o der Cousin (cousin, same as *der Vetter*)
- o der Delphin (larger sea mammals tend to be masculine)
- o der Harlekin (harlequin)
- o der Kamin (fireplace/chimney, same as *der Schornstein*)

o der Rosmarin (spices tend to be masculine)
o der Termin (from the Latin for *der Grenzstein*, and also meaning *der Zeitpunkt*)
o der Urin (because waste products tend to be masculine; the original word was also masculine: der Harn)

Exceptions (neuter nouns ending on -*in*; often chemical substances):

o das Adrenalin
o das Benzin
o das Cholesterin
o das Hämoglobin
o das Heroin
o das Insulin
o das Toxin

-itis/-tis: Medical terms, such as die Appendizitis, die Arthritis, die Gastroenteritis, die Konjunktivitis, die Meningitis, die Parodontitis, die Sinusitis. Two continents with this ending are feminine: die Arktis, die Antarktis

-keit: die Möglichkeit, die Schnelligkeit, die Schwierigkeit, die Unzulänglichkeit (inadequacy/deficiency)

-logie: die Biologie, die Meteorologie

-t: Nouns ending on -*t* derived from verbs

o die Ankunft (ankommen)
o die Arbeit (arbeiten)
o die Fahrt (fahren)
o die Geburt (gebären)
o die Haft (haften)
o die Schrift (schreiben)
o die Sicht (sehen)
o die Tat (tun)

Some single-syllable feminine nouns ending on -*t*:

o die Faust (fist; same feminine category as *die Hand*)
o die Flut (same feminine category as *die Strömung, die Überschwemmung, die Ebbe, die Wassermasse*)
o die Frist (time limit; many nouns about time and limits are feminine)
o die Front (same feminine category as *die Vorderseite, die Gefechtslinie*)
o die Haft (same category as *die Gefangenschaft, die Beschlagnahme, die Gefangennahme, die Fesselung*)
o die Haut (same category as *die Schale, die Umhüllung*)
o die Not (same category as *die Schwierigkeit, die Bedrängnis*)
o die Pest (from *die Pestilenz*, same category as *die Epidemie, die Plage, die Seuche, die Qual*)
o die Welt (same category as *die Erde, die Erdkugel*)
o die Wut (same category as *die Raserei, die Erregung*)

Exceptions (neuter): das Blut (blood), das Fett (nouns ending on -*ett* tend to be neuter), das Nest (same neuter category as *das Heim, das Bett*); Exceptions (masculine): der Geist (which makes all three persons of the Trinity masculine: der Vater, der Sohn und der Heilige Geist); der Test, der Rest

-ft: Nouns ending on -*ft* are likely to be feminine in the majority of cases: die Haft, die Kraft, die Luft, die Vernunft; given that words starting with *G*- tend to be neuter, it is perhaps not too surprising that one exception would be *das Gift*

-cht: Nouns ending on -*cht* are feminine 64 per cent of the time.[54]

o die Absicht (intention)
o die Acht (numbers are feminine)
o die Bucht (bay)

- o die Drogensucht (drug addiction)
- o die Eifersucht (jealousy)
- o die Eintracht (harmony)
- o die Fettsucht (obesity)
- o die Fracht (freight/cargo/load/carriage)
- o die Gefallsucht (flirtatious behaviour)
- o die Gelbsucht (jaundice)
- o die Gewinnsucht (excessive greediness)
- o die Habsucht (greed)
- o die Ichsucht (egotism)
- o die Macht (power/strength/might)
- o die Magersucht (anorexia)
- o die Nacht (night/night-time; similar feminine category as *die Dunkelheit, die Finsternis, die Düsterkeit*)
- o die Pflicht (obligation/duty/liability/task)
- o die Pracht (magnificence/splendour/glory)
- o die Sehnsucht (longing/desire/yearning)
- o die Selbstsucht (selfishness)
- o die Sicht (view/point of view/perspective)
- o die Spielsucht (addicted to gambling/compulsive gambling)
- o die Streitsucht (quarrelsomeness)
- o die Sucht (addiction)
- o die Tobsucht (raving madness)
- o die Trunksucht (alcoholism)
- o die Wassersucht (medical condition: hydrops)

Nouns ending on *-cht* are masculine 22 per cent of the time, and usually relate to persons: der Wicht (goblin/gnome), der Bösewicht (villain).

Nouns ending on *-cht* are neuter 15 per cent of the time, especially in cases where the noun refers to inanimate objects and/or starts with *Ge-*: das Gesicht (face).

-orm: die Form (from which: die Anredeform, die Plattform, die Reform, die Staatsform, die Uniform); die Norm

-tät: die Aktivität, die Elektrizität, die Identität, die Integrität, die Kapazität, die Lokalität, die Majestät, die Marktvolatilität, die Nationalität, die Pietät, die Priorität, die Qualität, die Universität

-thek: die Bibliothek, die Diskothek

-gion, -lion, -nion, -sion, -tion, -xion: die Religion, die Million, die Union, die Diskussion, die Mission, die Funktion, die Koalition, die Nation, die Situation, die Reflexion

-schaft: This is the German equivalent of English words ending on *-ship*, as in friendship/*Freundschaft* or *-hood*, as in brotherhood/*Bruderschaft*

- die Botschaft (embassy/message)
- die Bruderschaft (brotherhood/fraternity)
- die Eigenschaft (characteristic/property/feature/quality)
- die Freundschaft
- die Genossenschaft (cooperative)
- die Gesellschaft
- die Hiobsbotschaft (bad news/evil tidings)
- die Herrschaft (rule/control/domination/dominion)
- die Mannschaft (team/crew/squad/side)
- die Seilschaft (old boys' network)
- die Wirtschaft

-sis: die Basis, die Dosis, die Genesis, die Katharsis, die Skepsis

-ung: (nouns ending on *-ung*, especially if they contain more than one syllable, are very likely to be feminine)

- die Abteilung
- die Abwägung (e.g. *die Kosten-Nutzen-Abwägung*)
- die Anlegerstimmung
- die Bedeutung

- o die Bedingung
- o die Beobachtung
- o die Beratung
- o die Bewegung
- o die Beziehung
- o die Bildung
- o die Einführung
- o die Endung
- o die Erfahrung
- o die Erfindung
- o die Erklärung
- o die Erzählung
- o die Erziehung
- o die Forschung
- o die Handlung
- o die Landung
- o die Leistung
- o die Leitung
- o die Lösung
- o die Neigung
- o die Öffnung
- o die Ordnung
- o die Prüfung
- o die Regierung
- o die Rettung
- o die Richtung
- o die Sammlung
- o die Sendung
- o die Siedlung
- o die Spannung
- o die Stimmung
- o die Übung
- o die Veränderung
- o die Verbindung
- o die Verfolgung
- o die Verletzung
- o die Vorlesung

o die Währung
o die Warnung
o die Werbung
o die Wirkung
o die Zeichnung
o die Zeitung
o die Wohnung

Given that the majority of one-syllable nouns tend to be masculine, we also find a few one-syllable masculine exceptions to the feminine -ung rule:

o der Dung (dung/manure/muck)
o der Schwung (and hence also new nouns created with this one-syllable masculine root, such as, *der Aufschwung*, *der Umschwung*)
o der Sprung (and for the same reason as above, *der Absprung, der Ursprung*)

-ur: (but not -eur[55]) Nouns ending on -ur or -ür are feminine 93 per cent of the time.[56]

o die Agentur
o die Armatur (fitting/fixture)
o die Frisur
o die Glasur
o die Kultur
o die Literatur
o die Natur
o die Reparatur
o die Spur
o die Tastatur
o die Temperatur

Exceptions (masculine, five per cent of the time): der Merkur (Mercury, same broader category as *der Mars*, *der Saturn*, *der Jupiter* and *der Neptun*)

Exceptions (neuter, around two per cent of the time): das Abitur (imported from the Latin *Abiturium*)

-ür: die Tür, die Willkür (but *das* Gespür because nouns starting with *Ge-* tend to be neuter)

Das: The rules that make nouns neuter

Rule 1: Categories

References to higher-level or first-order categories of things, or collections of inanimate things, are often neuter: (see Figure 1 in the Introduction for a schematic depiction of this principle)

- das All/das Universum: The universe is neuter; its many sub-components have all three genders
- das Alter/das Altertum/das Altsein
- das Besteck: der Löffel, die Gabel, das Messer
- das Ding
- das Erzeugnis: das Glaserzeugnis
- das Fleisch
- das Gerät
- das Gesicht: der Mund, die Nase, das Ohr
- das Geflügel (poultry): der Hahn, die Henne, das Küken
- das Getränk: der Wein, der Saft
- das Gewürz: der Pfeffer, das Salz
- das Gut: das Massengut, das Kulturgut, das Landgut
- das Insekt
- das Instrument
- das Kleid: das Abendkleid, das Brautkleid
- das Mahl: das Essen
- das Mehl
- das Material
- das Obst
- das Pferd

- das Produkt: das Agrarprodukt, das Industrieprodukt
- das Rind: der Bulle, die Kuh, das Kälbchen
- das Schiff/das Boot
- das Tier
- das Wild (venison)
- das Wort
- das Zeug: das Werkzeug

Letters of the alphabet: das A, das B, including das Eszett (the letter ß)

Languages are usually neuter: das Deutsch, das Englisch, das Latein

Some grammatical terms/parts of speech: das Adjektiv, das Attribut, das Futur (future tense), das Perfekt (perfect tense), das Präfix, das Präteritum (past tense), das Nomen, das Substantiv, das Suffix, das Verb, das Wort, das Komma

Exceptions: grammatical cases (because they are part of the masculine category for "case": *der Kasus, der Fall*), such as *der Nominativ, der Akkusativ, der Dativ, der Infinitiv, der Superlativ*

Nouns derived from infinitives: das Essen, das Schreiben, das Laufen, das Schwimmen

Nouns derived from adjectives: (without referring to a specific person or thing) das Gute, das Böse, das Schöne, das Ungeheure (enormous, immense, vast), das Neue, das Gleiche, das Ganze

Colours: das Blau, das Rot, das Gelb, das Hellgrün, das Dunkelbraun, das Lila/das Violett (note that some colours have the same name as another object with another gender, for example turquoise, *das Türkis*, which is greenish-blue, and is named after the gemstone *der Türkis*)

Names of continents, countries, regions, cities and valleys are neuter in the vast majority of cases. Usually, the neuter identifier "das" is *not* placed in front of a country or city name, but it becomes relevant in certain contexts. For example: "*Das heutige Italien hat Wirtschaftsprobleme.*" Countries with the ending *-ien*, *-land*, *-reich* or *-stan* are always neuter. Examples: Italien, Spanien, Deutschland, England, Österreich, Frankreich, Vereinigtes Königreich, Afghanistan, Pakistan.

Unlike in the case of neuter countries, the definite article for masculine and feminine countries is always used.

Countries with feminine names: die Schweiz, die Slowakei, die Türkei, die Mongolei, die Ukraine

Countries with masculine names: der Irak, der Iran, der Jemen, der Senegal, der Sudan, der Südsudan, der Niger, der Vatikan

For some inexplicable reason, the new state of Kosovo is both masculine and neuter.[57] A similar problem exists in the case of Oman, which can be *der* (used in Austria, Switzerland and southern Germany) or *das*.

Even though the noun for "city" (*die Stadt*) is feminine, the category "named city", is neuter. Just as in the example of neuter countries cited above, this neuter gender only reveals itself with the help of an adjective: *das* geteilte Berlin. This neuter category (Rule 1) is powerful enough to override the implicit gender of the noun ending (Rule 2). For example, it is "*das* mittelalterliche Hamburg", even though the ending *-burg* is feminine: *die* Burg (from *die Festung*, *die Stadt*).

There is a similar principle when it comes to the continents. The noun for continent is masculine: *der Kontinent*, which is the synonym of *der Erdteil* (a vast area of land mass). But, when we name the continents individually, they have their own gender. *Arktis* and *Antarktis* are feminine, whereas *Afrika*, *Amerika*,

Asien, Europa and *Ozeanien* are neuter. The way that the gender of a neuter continent reveals itself is with the help of an adjective: *"das* ferne Asien" or *"das* alte Europa". Only in the case of the feminine continents must the definite article be used: "Wir besuchen *die* Arktis."

The same principle applies to islands. The noun for island is feminine (*die Insel*), however, the names of islands, especially if they are also countries, tend to be neuter: *das* schöne Mauritius, *das* kommunistische Kuba

Human and animal babies:[58] das Baby, das Kind, das Kalb, das Kälbchen, das Ferkel, das Küken, das Lamm

Diminutives: (*-chen, -lein,* and their dialect forms *-le, -erl, -el, -li*) das Kaninchen, das Fräulein, das Aschenbrödel; Haus → das Häuschen, das Häuslein

Pieces and tiny particles: das Stück, das Teil, das Atom, das Molekül, das Elektron, das Neutron, das Gen (gene)

Almost all of the 112 known elements of the Periodic Table: das Aluminium, das Kupfer, das Uran (six exceptions: der Kohlenstoff, der Sauerstoff, der Stickstoff, der Wasserstoff, der Phosphor, der Schwefel)

Names of metals: das Blei, das Messing (brass), das Zinn (exceptions: die Bronze, der Stahl)

Materials: das Glas, das Holz

Fire and water: das Feuer, das Wasser

Grass: das Gras, das Haschisch, das Marihuana, das Heu, das Viehfutter, das Kraut (herb/kraut/cabbage), das Unkraut (weed)

Units of measurement in physics: das Ampere, das Ohm, das Watt, das Volt, das Newton

Units of measurement of temperature: das Celsius, das Fahrenheit, das Kelvin

Units of weight: das Gewicht, das Pfund, das Kilogramm (unless the noun has the feminine -e ending: *die Tonne, die Unze*)

The measure or extent of something, or the unit used for measuring: das Mass (meaning amount, degree, measure, measurement, dosage, gage); from which follows *das Ausmass* (the extent or dimension of something)

Musical tones: das Dur (major key), das Moll (minor key)

- Some musical settings: das Konzert, das Orchester, das Theater, das Ballett (but *die* Oper, *die* Band)

- Some musical instruments not ending on -*e:* das Cello, das Cembalo, das Klavier, das Piano

Fractions: das Drittel (⅓), das Viertel (¼), das Quartal (exception: die Hälfte); $^1/_{20}$ → das Zwanzigstel (the Swiss disagree, and classify all fractions ending on -*tel* as masculine)

Books/paper/written minutes: das Wort, das Buch, das Papier, das Blatt, das Dokument, das Protokoll, das Kapitel

Types of sport and games:

- das Aerobic
- das Backgammon
- das Badminton
- das Bowling
- das Golf

o das Hockey
o das Jogging
o das Karate
o das Pilates
o das Poker
o das Schach (chess)
o das Schwimmen
o das Squash
o das Tennis
o das Turnen (gymnastics)
o das Yoga

Exceptions: compound nouns ending on *der Ball* (as in *der Fussball*) or *der Sport* (as in *der Motorsport, der Wassersport*)

Medicine: das Medikament/das Heilmittel/das Arzneimittel → das Aspirin (generic name)

Detergents: das Waschmittel → das Ariel, das Omo, das Vim, das Persil

Names of hotels, cafés, clubs, theatres, movie houses: das Hilton, das Odeon

Foreign words imported into German tend to become neuter, e.g. *das Know-how.* The exceptions tend to occur when the Germans already have a noun in another gender for the same word. For example, *die Holding*, as in a holding company, for which they already had *die Firma/die Gesellschaft*

Rule 2: Sounds

-aar: das Haar, das Paar, but *die Saar*, a river in Europe (Rule 1: categories)

-är: das Militär, das Salär

-al:

- o das Denkmal
- o das Festival
- o das Ideal
- o das Kapital
- o das Lokal
- o das Oval
- o das Pedal
- o das Personal
- o das Portal
- o das Schicksal
- o das Signal
- o das Spital
- o das Tal

Exeptions: die Moral (similar to *die Ethik, die Sittlichkeit*), der Karneval (similar to *der Fasching*), der Schal, der Kanal (similar to *der Wasserlauf, der Wasserweg, der Sund*)

-at:

- o das Aggregat (unit/set)
- o das Attentat
- o das Dekanat (office of the dean)
- o das Derivat
- o das Destillat
- o das Diktat
- o das Dirigat
- o das Duplikat
- o das Emirat
- o das Exponat (exhibit)
- o das Fabrikat (make/brand/manufactured product)
- o das Filtrat

- das Format
- das Implantat (implant)
- das Inserat (advertisement)
- das Internat (boarding school)
- das Kalifat
- das Kondensat
- das Konglomerat
- das Konkordat
- das Konsulat
- das Korrelat
- das Laminat
- das Lektorat (editorial office at a publisher)
- das Mandat
- das Nitrat
- das Opiat
- das Phosphat
- das Plagiat
- das Plakat
- das Postulat
- das Proletariat/das Lumpenproletariat
- das Protektorat
- das Quadrat
- das Referat
- das Rektorat
- das Syndikat
- das Unikat (one-off/something unique)
- das Zertifikat
- das Zitat

Masculine exceptions in the *-at* category tend to be nouns that refer to a masculine person, profession or function. If the noun refererred to a woman in such a role, the ending *-in* would typically be added:

- der Advokat
- der Akrobat
- der Aristokrat

- o der Bürokrat
- o der Demokrat
- o der Diplomat
- o der Pirat
- o der Renegat
- o der Soldat

or nouns that refer to machines, equipment, tools:

- o der Apparat
- o der Automat
- o der Thermostat (but in this case, it can also be *das*)

And numerous derivatives of the noun *der Rat* (which, in its original sense referred to all kinds of provisioning, but today means advice, council), such as *der Beirat* (advisory board or council), *der Sicherheitsrat* (Security Council), which would also explain the masculine gender of *der Senat* (a council of elders); other masculine nouns in this category include *der Hausrat* (furniture, or provisioning for the home), *der Vorrat* (provisions, supplies, stocks), and *der Verrat* (which appears to be the opposite of honest provisioning: treason, betrayal, treachery).

Exceptions that are feminine include nouns associated with feminine categories, e.g. *die Kumquat* (fruit tends to be feminine), *die Tat* (same category as *die Aktion, die Handlung*), *die Zutat* (ingredient; because the root noun *Tat* is feminine), *die Heimat* (home country) and *die Heirat* (marriage, another kind of provisioning for the home, and that noun is in the same feminine category as other words for marriage: *die Ehe, die Eheschliessung, die Hochzeit, die Trauung, die Verheiratung*).

-bot:

- o das Angebot (offer)
- o das Aufgebot (contingent/military call-up)

- o das Ausgehverbot (curfew/confinement to barracks/grounding)
- o das Gebot (bid/requirement/order/law)
- o das Überangebot (oversupply)

Exception: In computing, a bot in German is *der Bot* because the noun originates from *der Roboter.*

-eil: das Seil, das Urteil, das Gegenteil

Das Teil (*loses Stück/*a loose piece of something): das Puzzleteil, das Ersatzteil, das Einzelteil, das Oberteil, das Plastikteil, das Wrackteil

*Der Teil (Teil eines Ganzen/*an integral part of a whole): der Erdteil, der Landesteil, der Stadtteil, der Elternteil (parent), der Bestandteil, der (vordere/hintere) Zugteil, der Mittelteil (such as the middle part of a book)

-em: Nouns that end on *-em* and are stressed on the last syllable are often imported words (from Greek origin), which would tend to make them neuter.

- o das Diadem
- o das Ekzem
- o das Emblem
- o das Extrem
- o das Ödem
- o das Phonem
- o das Problem
- o das System
- o das Theorem

Also, the following nouns with the stress on the first syllable are neuter: das Modem, das Requiem, das Totem, das Tandem (bicycle with two seats)

But the following nouns with the stress on the first syllable are masculine: der Atem, der Harem, der Moslem

-ett: Nouns that end on *-ett* are neuter 95 per cent of the time.[59]

o das Bajonett
o das Ballett
o das Bankett
o das Billett
o das Brikett
o das Büffett
o das Bukett
o das Duett
o das Eszett (the letter ß)
o das Etikett
o das Flageolett
o das Florett
o das Flötenquartett
o das Flussbett
o das Inlett
o das Jackett
o das Kabarett
o das Kabinett
o das Kabriolett
o das Klosett
o das Kornett
o das Körperfett
o das Korsett
o das Kotelett
o das Kriegskabinett
o das Lazarett
o das Menuett
o das Minarett
o das Oktett
o das Omelett
o das Parkett
o das Quartett

- o das Rechenbrett
- o das Reissbrett
- o das Roulett
- o das Schachbrett
- o das Servierbrett
- o das Sextett
- o das Skelett
- o das Sonett
- o das Spinett
- o das Sprungbrett
- o das Stilett
- o das Surfbrett
- o das Tablett
- o das Violett
- o das Zeichenbrett

-euer: das Feuer, das Abenteuer, das Ungeheuer

-fon/-phon: das Telefon, das Mikrophon, das Megaphon, das Grammophon, das Saxofon/Saxophon, das Xylofon/Xylophon

Ge-: Nouns that begin with the unstressed syllable *Ge-* and do not mean a person are often neuter, e.g. das Gehirn (the brain). Also, nouns created from *Ge-* + verb root + *-e* are always neuter: fragen → das Gefrage (questions), bauen → das Gebäude, malen → das Gemälde, as well as most nouns constructed in this way from closely related nouns, e.g. (Berge → das Gebirge)

- o das Gebäck
- o das Gebäude
- o das Gebell
- o das Gebet
- o das Gebiet
- o das Gebirge
- o das Gebiss (bit for a horse/dentures)
- o das Gedächtnis

- das Gedicht
- das Gefäss
- das Gefühl
- das Gehäuse
- das Geheimnis
- das Geheiss (*das Gebot*, at someone's behest or bidding)
- das Gehirn
- das Gejaule (howling)
- das Gelaber (jabbering/bantering/talking drivel)
- das Gelächter (laughter)
- das Gelage (feast/banquet/revelry/binge)
- das Gelände
- das Gelenk (joint)
- das Gemälde (painting)
- das Gemäuer (masonry/walls/ruins)
- das Gemenge
- das Gemetzel (bloodbath/slaughter/massacre)
- das Gemüse
- das Gemüt (disposition)
- das Genick
- das Gepäck
- das Gerangel (wrangle/dispute)
- das Gerät
- das Geräusch
- das Gerede
- das Gericht
- das Gerinnsel
- das Gerippe
- das Geröll
- das Gerücht
- das Gerümpel
- das Gerüst
- das Gesäss
- das Geschäft
- das Geschehen
- das Geschenk
- das Geschick

- das Geschirr
- das Geschlecht
- das Geschöpf
- das Geschoss
- das Geschrei
- das Geschütz
- das Geschwader
- das Geschwätz
- das Geschwür
- das Gesetz
- das Gesicht
- das Gesindel
- das Gespenst
- das Gespräch
- das Gespür
- das Gestein
- das Gestell
- das Gestirn
- das Gestrüpp
- das Gestüt
- das Gesuch
- das Getöse (roar/noise/din)
- das Getränk
- das Getreide
- das Getue
- das Gewächs
- das Gewand
- das Gewässer
- das Gewebe
- das Gewehr
- das Geweih
- das Gewerbe
- das Gewicht
- das Gewieher (neighing/horse laugh)
- das Gewinde (the threads on a screw)
- das Gewirr
- das Gewissen

- o das Gewitter
- o das Gewölbe
- o das Gewühl
- o das Gewürz

Exceptions:

Masculine nouns starting with *Ge-* tend to be more abstract than neuter nouns starting with *Ge-*:

- o der Gebrauch
- o der Gedanke
- o der Genuss
- o der Geruch
- o der Gesang
- o der Geschmack
- o der Gestank
- o der Gewinn

Feminine nouns starting with *Ge-* also tend to be more abstract than neuter nouns starting with *Ge-*:

- o die Gebärde (gesture: movements tend to be feminine)
- o die Gebühr (fee: payments and taxes are feminine)
- o die Geburt
- o die Geduld
- o die Gefahr
- o die Gemeinde
- o die Geschichte (history: story-telling and speech acts are feminine)
- o die Gestalt (form/shape or figure)
- o die Gewähr (warranty)
- o die Gewalt (force/authority or violence)

-gramm:

- o das Anagramm
- o das Autogramm
- o das Diagramm
- o das Hologramm
- o das Kilogramm
- o das Mikrogramm
- o das Milligramm
- o das Monogramm
- o das Parallelogramm
- o das Programm
- o das Seismogramm
- o das Telegramm

-horn:

- o das Alphorn (musical instrument)
- o das Eichhorn/Eichhörnchen (squirrel)
- o das Einhorn (unicorn)
- o das Füllhorn (cornucopia/horn of plenty)
- o das Greenhorn/Grünhorn (greenhorn/novice)
- o das Hirschhorn (deer antler)
- o das Horn (horn/bump/lump/bugle/hooter)
- o das Matterhorn (name of a mountain in the Alps)
- o das Nashorn (rhinoceros)

Exception: der Ahorn (maple tree; trees tend not to be neuter)

-ial: das Material, das Potenzial

-iel:

- o das Beispiel (example)
- o das Endspiel (the finals)
- o das Glücksspiel (gamble/gambling)

- o das Lustspiel (commedy)
- o das Spiel (game/match)
- o das Trauerspiel (tragedy/fiasco)
- o das Ziel (target)

-ier: Nounds ending on *-ier* are neuter 60 per cent of the time, masculine 30 per cent and feminine 10 per cent.[60]

When a noun ending on *-ier* does not refer to persons, e.g. der Australier, der Bankier, der Brigadier, or to specific types of animals, e.g. der Dinosaurier, der Stier, der Yorkshireterrier, but to inanimate things or higher-level categories of things, then the *-ier* ending usually indicates a neuter noun:

- o das Atelier (studio)
- o das Bier
- o das Elixier
- o das Klavier
- o das Metier (profession/trade)
- o das Papier
- o das Quartier
- o das Tier
- o das Turnier (tournament)
- o das Visier (visor/gunsight)

Given that feminine tends to be the default gender for abstract nouns, this would explain *die Gier* (greed, lust, avarice). Another rare feminine noun ending on *-ier* is *die Feier* (celebration, ceremony, festival).

-ing: Nouns imported from English with the ending *-ing* are usually neuter.

- o das Babysitting
- o das Bodybuilding
- o das Bowling
- o das Brainstorming

- o das Branding
- o das Camping
- o das Controlling
- o das Desktoppublishing
- o das Dribbling
- o das Doping
- o das Dressing
- o das Jogging
- o das Lobbying
- o das Marketing
- o das Mobbing
- o das Recycling
- o das Stalking
- o das Training

Exceptions: When similar nouns or noun-endings exist in German, then they typically take the gender of the existing German word.

Feminine nouns ending on *-ing*:

- o die Holding (same category as *die Firma, die Gesellschaft*)

Masculine nouns ending on *-ing*:

- o der Boxring (masculine because of the ending: *der Ring* and a German synomym existed: *der Kampfplatz*)

-ip: das Prinzip (and its many compound forms: das Autoritätsprinzip, das Einteilungsprinzip, das Fertigungsprinzip, das Grundprinzip, das Kausalprinzip, das Lebensprinzip, das Leistungsprinzip, das Leitungsprinzip, das Majoritätsprinzip, das Moralprinzip, das Nützlichkeitsprinzip, das Ordnungsprinzip, das Prioritätsprinzip, das Relativitätsprinzip, das Sparsamkeitsprinzip)

-iv:

- o das Additiv
- o das Adjektiv
- o das Archiv
- o das Leitmotiv
- o das Motiv
- o das Präservativ

(Exceptions: grammatical *cases*, because they belong to the category *der Kasus*, *der Fall*: der Nominativ, der Akkusativ, der Dativ, der Infinitiv, der Superlativ)

-lein: (these diminutives tend to appear in idiomatic or more picturesque language) das Bächlein, das Büchlein, das Fräulein, das Gänslein, das Knäblein, das Krüglein, das Männlein, das Scherflein, das Stiftsfräulein, das Stündlein, das Vöglein, das Zicklein, das Zünglein

-ld: das Bild, das Geld, das Gold, das Umfeld, das Spielfeld, das Erdölfeld, das Mittelfeld, das Spannungsfeld, das Trümmerfeld, das Magnetfeld, das Schild (same category as *das Plakat*), das Wild

Masculine: der Held, der Schild, der Sold, der Wald

Feminine: die Geduld, die Schuld

-ma: (of Greek origin)

- o das Aroma
- o das Charisma
- o das Dilemma
- o das Dogma
- o das Drama
- o das Klima
- o das Koma (coma)

- das Komma (comma)
- das Magma
- das Panorama
- das Paradigma
- das Plasma
- das Prisma
- das Schema
- das Sperma
- das Stigma
- das Thema
- das Trauma

Not of Greek origin: das Karma, das Lama

Exceptions: *die Firma* (same category as *die Gesellschaft*), *der Puma* (scary animals tend to be masculine)

-ment: Quite a few imported foreign nouns in this category, and imported words, tend to be neuter.

- das Abonnement
- das Apartment
- das Argument
- das Departement
- das Dokument
- das Element
- das Equipment
- das Experiment
- das Fragment
- das Fundament
- das Instrument
- das Kompliment
- das Management
- das Medikament
- das Monument
- das Ornament
- das Parlament

- das Pergament
- das Pigment
- das Posament
- das Regiment
- das Reglement
- das Sakrament
- das Sediment
- das Segment
- das Sortiment
- das Statement
- das Temperament
- das Testament
- das Wealth Management

Exceptions:

- der Konsument (consumer; relates to a person, whereas the above neuter nouns do not)
- der Zement (same category as *der Sand, der Stein, der Beton, der Kiesel, der Kitt, der Klebstoff*)

-nis: Nouns with the ending *-nis* are either neuter or feminine.

Feminine nouns ending on *-nis* tend to refer to attitudes, conditions or to more abstract concepts:

- die Bedrängnis (distress; similar category as *die Angst, die Sorge* and other existential conditions, such as *die Armut*)
- die Befugnis (authorization)
- die Bewandtnis (unique feature/ quality/condition/state/aspect/characteristic)
- die Bitternis (bitterness/hardship)
- die Empfängnis (conception)
- die Erlaubnis (permission; in this category we also find rules and limits: die Regelung, die Frist, die Limitierung, die Grenze, die Begrenzung, die Beschränkung)
- die Ersparnis (savings or the act of saving)

o die Fäulnis (rot/decay)
o die Finsternis (darkness/eclipse; similar category as *die Dunkelheit, die Nacht*)
o die Kenntnis (knowledge/awareness; wisdom is a feminine category)
o die Wildnis (hunting is feminine, after the female Greek and Roman godesses of hunting)

Neuter nouns ending on *-nis* tend to refer to somewhat more concrete things (events/outcomes/physical things):

o das Ärgernis (pain in the neck/nuisance)
o das Bedürfnis (requirement/necessity)
o das Begräbnis (funeral/burial)
o das Bekenntnis (commitment/confession/faith)
o das Besäufnis (boozing)
o das Bildnis (image/portrait/effigy)
o das Bündnis (alliance/league/confederacy)
o das Eingeständnis (confession)
o das Ereignis (event/incident)
o das Ergebnis (outcome; also for business: das Betriebsergebnis)
o das Erlebnis (experience/adventure; also in a break-through sense: das Aha-Erlebnis)
o das Erzeugnis (product)
o das Gedächtnis (memory/mind/commemoration; the brain is neuter too: das Gehirn)
o das Gefängnis (prison)
o das Geheimnis (similar category as *das Rätsel, das Mysterium, das Phänomen, das Wunder*)
o das Geständnis (confession/admission: similar category to *das Bekenntnis,* above)
o das Hemmnis (sometimes a subtler kind of obstacle/barrier/impediment/hindrance)
o das Hindernis (sometimes a more physical kind of obstacle/barrier/impediment/hindrance)
o das Missverständnis (misunderstanding)

- das Tennis (types of sport tend to be neuter)
- das Unverständnis (incomprehension)
- das Verhältnis (e.g. *das Risiko-Rendite-Verhältnis*)
- das Verhängnis (doom/fate/downfall)
- das Verständnis (understanding)
- das Verzeichnis (list/directory/inventory)
- das Wagnis (risk/venture/hazzard)
- das Zerwürfnis (quarrel/row/discord)
- das Zeugnis (testimony/certificate/reference)

-ol: In this category, we tend to find many chemical substances, which are usually neuter, as well as the frequently used words *das Idol* and *das Symbol*.

- das Aerosol
- das Äthanol/Ethanol
- das Benzol
- das Cobol
- das Glykol
- das Idol
- das Menthol
- das Mol
- das Monopol
- das Phenol
- das Polystyrol
- das Sol (a chemical; the Roman sun god would be *der*)
- das Stanniol
- das Südtirol (countries and regions tend to be neuter)
- das Symbol
- das Thymol
- das Tirol (countries and regions tend to be neuter)
- das Toluol

Exceptions:

- der Alkohol (while chemicals tend to be neuter, alcohol and alcoholic drinks tend to be masculine)

- o der Pirol (a kind of bird; birds tend to be masculine)
- o der Pol, der Nordpol, der Südpol, der Gegenpol (points on the compass are masculine)

-om/-ym:

- o das Akronym
- o das Atom
- o das Axiom
- o das Binom
- o das Chromosom
- o das Diplom
- o das Enzym
- o das Genom
- o das Kondom
- o das Metronom
- o das Monom
- o das Phantom
- o das Polynom
- o das Pseudonym
- o das Symptom
- o das Syndrom

-skop:

- o das Horoskop
- o das Kaleidoskop
- o das Mikroskop
- o das Periskop
- o das Stethoskop
- o das Teleskop

-tum:

- o das Altertum
- o das Analphabetentum (illiteracy)
- o das Arboretum

o das Ausstellungsdatum
o das Bauerntum
o das Besitztum
o das Bevölkerungswachstum
o das Bistum
o das Brauchtum
o das Bürgertum
o das Christentum
o das Datum
o das Diktum
o das Eigentum
o das Erratum
o das Erzbistum
o das Erzherzogtum
o das Faktum
o das Fürstentum
o das Geldmengenwachstum
o das Gemeindeeigentum
o das Gewinnwachstum
o das Grossherzogtum
o das Grundeigentum
o das Haltbarkeitsdatum
o das Heidentum
o das Heiligtum
o das Heldentum
o das Herstelldatum
o das Importwachstum
o das Jahreswachstum
o das Judentum
o das Kaisertum
o das Kleinbürgertum
o das Kompositum (compound)
o das Künstlertum
o das Laientum
o das Lieferdatum
o das Mehrheitsvotum
o das Misstrauensvotum

- o das Miteigentum
- o das Mitläufertum
- o das Mönchstum
- o das Nullwachstum
- o das Papsttum
- o das Präteritum (past tense)
- o das Privateigentum
- o das Quantum
- o das Rektum
- o das Scheichtum
- o das Skrotum
- o das Stadtbürgertum
- o das Strebertum (nerdishness)
- o das Tagesdatum
- o das Ultimatum
- o das Unternehmertum
- o das Verbrechertum
- o das Verfalldatum
- o das Vertrauensvotum
- o das Volkstum
- o das Votum
- o das Wachstum
- o das Wirtschaftswachstum
- o das Zellwachstum
- o das Zwittertum

Exceptions:

- o der Irrtum (same category as *der Fehler*)
- o der Reichtum

-um: (especially if the noun is of Latin origin)

- o das Album
- o das Aquarium
- o das Auditorium
- o das Bakterium

- o das Evangelium
- o das Forum
- o das Gymnasium
- o das Impressum
- o das Individuum
- o das Jubiläum
- o das Kriterium
- o das Maximum
- o das Minimum
- o das Ministerium
- o das Museum
- o das Opium
- o das Optimum
- o das Pensum (workload)
- o das Podium
- o das Publikum
- o das Serum
- o das Stadium
- o das Studium
- o das Vakuum
- o das Visum
- o das Zentrum

Exception: der Konsum (same category as *der Verbrauch*)

-werk: Compound nouns from *das Werk*

- o das Atomkraftwerk
- o das Bauwerk
- o das Bollwerk
- o das Braunkohlekraftwerk
- o das Breitbandnetzwerk
- o das Computernetzwerk
- o das Dampfkraftwerk
- o das Datennetzwerk
- o das Diskettenlaufwerk
- o das Erdwärmekraftwerk

- o das Feuerwerk
- o das Gaskraftwerk
- o das Gaswerk
- o das Gedankenwerk
- o das Gemeinschaftswerk
- o das Gewerk (trade or craft)
- o das Glaswerk
- o das Handwerk
- o das Hauptwerk
- o das Hilfswerk
- o das Kraftwerk
- o das Kunstwerk
- o das Laufwerk
- o das Meisterwerk
- o das Metallwerk
- o das Nachschlagewerk
- o das Netzwerk
- o das Orchesterwerk
- o das Sammelwerk
- o das Stahlwerk
- o das Standardwerk
- o das Stockwerk
- o das Strahltriebwerk
- o das Wasserwerk
- o das Windkraftwerk
- o das Wunderwerk

-yl:

- o das Acryl
- o das Asyl (asylum, from the Greek, and as an imported word would thus tend to be neuter)
- o das Vinyl

-zept:

- das Konzept
- das Rezept

-zeug:

- das Zeug
- das Fahrzeug
- das Flugzeug
- das Kampfflugzeug
- das Militärflugzeug
- das Passagierflugzeug
- das Schreibzeug
- das Silberzeug
- das Spielzeug
- das Werkzeug

One or the other

In cases where nouns tend to be associated with only two of the three genders, you have a higher chance of guessing the correct gender.

Masculine or neuter

Nouns that end with a double consonant, such as *-ck*, *-tz* or *-ss*, are usually masculine or neuter if they do not end with *-ness* (e.g. die Fitness, die Wellness).

One way to try and make the distinction between masculine and neuter words in this category is that nouns starting with *G-* or *Ge-* tend to be neuter.

-ck:

Masculine: der Blick, der Dreck, der Druck, der Fleck, der Geck, der Klick, der Knick (kink/bend/buckling/crease), der Lack (varnish), der Rock, der Schluck, der Speck, der Trick, der Zweck

Neuter: das Dreieck (triangle), das Gebäck (words beginning with *Ge-* tend to be neuter), das Genick (back of the neck), das Gepäck, das Glück, das Stück, das Comeback, das Feedback (imported words tend to be neuter)

-eer: das Heer (army), das Meer (sea), der Lorbeer (laurel/bay leaf), der Teer (tar), der Speer (spear), der Eritreer (Eritrean)

-isch:

Masculine nouns ending on *-isch:* der Fisch, der Tisch, der Fetisch

Neuter nouns ending on *-isch* include languages; and languages as a category tend to be neuter: *das Arabisch, das Englisch, das Spanisch*

-kt:

Masculine: der Affekt (affect, emotion), der Akt, der Architekt, der Aspekt, der Defekt, der Dialekt, der Effekt, der Infarkt, der Infekt, der Instinkt, der Intellekt, der Katarakt (waterfall), der Konflikt, der Kontakt, der Kontrakt, der Markt, der Pakt, der Prospekt, der Punkt, der Respekt, der Sekt, der Takt, der Trakt

Neuter: das Artefakt, das Delikt, das Edikt, das Konfekt, das Insekt, das Konstrukt, das Objekt, das Perfekt (the perfect tense in grammar, and grammatical terms tend to be neuter), das Projekt, das Produkt, das Relikt, das Subjekt, das Verdikt (same category as *das Urteil*)

Exception (feminine): *die* Katarakt (cataract of the eye; not to be confused with *der* Katarakt, a waterfall)

-o: Nouns that end on *-o* are usually neuter or masculine.

Examples (neuter):

of Greek origin (and imported words tend to be neuter): das Auto, das Kino, das Kilo, das Deo, das Trio, das Ego, das Foto,[61] das Echo, das Logo, das Mikro, das Makro

of Latin origin: das Video, das Credo/Kredo, das Neutrino, das Memo of French origin: das Abo (from *das Abonnement*), das Bistro, das Büro, das Cabrio, das Karo, das Portfolio, das Rokoko, das Rollo

of Italian origin: das Solo, das Duo, das Manko, das Tempo, das Motto, das Fresko, das Studio, das Ghetto, das Piano, das Kasino, das Konto, das Veto, das Lotto, das Porto, das Intermezzo, das Inferno, das Libretto, das Risiko, das Rondo, das Fiasko, das Inkasso, das Kommando, das Szenario, das Intro (opening musical piece)

of English origin: das Banjo, das Ufo, das Shampoo, das Bingo, das Placebo

of Spanish origin: das Embargo, das Lasso, das Eldorado

a language ending on -*o* (and languages tend to be neuter): das Esperanto

musical instruments ending on -*o*: das Cello, das Cembalo, das Piano

Types of sport ending on -*o* that are neuter: das Judo, das Polo, das Rodeo

Names of neuter countries ending on -*o*: (das alte) Montenegro, (das alte) Marokko, (das alte) Monaco, (das alte) Mexiko

Exceptions (masculine nouns ending on -*o*):

- o der Bolero (many dances are masculine)
- o der Cappuccino (drinks tend to be masculine)
- o der Dingo (same category as *der Hund*)
- o der Dynamo (most types of machinery are masculine)
- o der Embryo (same category as *der Fetus*, *der Keim*)
- o der Eskimo
- o der Espresso (drinks tend to be masculine)

o der Euro (many currencies are masculine)
o der Fango (mud used in treatments; the category soil is masculine)
o der Flamenco (dances tend to be masculine)
o der Flamingo (bigger birds tend to be masculine)
o der Gigolo
o der Gusto (same category as *der Geschmack*)
o der Kakao (drinks tend to be masculine)
o der Macho
o der Mungo (mongoose)
o der Oregano (spices tend to be masculine)
o der Pluto (the category "heavenly bodies" tends to be masculine)
o der Porno (because it is short for *der Pornofilm*)
o der Saldo (same category as *der Betrag, der Kontostand*)
o der Salto (same category as *der Überschlag*)
o der Schirokko (a kind of wind)
o der Sombrero (same category as *der Hut*)
o der Tacho (speedometer: most types of machinery and instruments are masculine)
o der Tango (dances tend to be masculine)
o der Torero (a bullfighter)
o der Tornado (types of wind tend to be masculine)
o der Torpedo (most types of machinery are masculine)
o der Torso (same category as *der Oberkörper*)
o der Trafo (transformer: most types of machinery are masculine)
o der Zoo (same category as *der Tiergarten*)

Exceptions (feminine): die Demo, die Disko, die Limo, die Info (because they are short for *die Demonstration, die Diskothek, die Limousine, die Information*); die Uno/UNO, die NATO, die NGO (because the *O* stands for *die Organisation*); die Avocado, die Mango (fruit tends to be feminine); die Libido

-os: This is a typical ending for many masculine Greek nouns and names; think, for example, of the Greek god of wine,

Dionysos. When imported into German though, Greek nouns ending on *-os* tend to remain masculine (*der Kosmos, der Mythos*) or they become neuter, as in the case of most imported words (*das Chaos, das Pathos*). The useful insight here is that at least German nouns ending on *-os* are not typically associated with feminine nouns.

-tz: der Blitz, der Schlitz, der Sitz, der Witz, der Platz, der Satz

Feminine or masculine

-mut: Nouns ending on *-mut* are to be found across all three genders, but the abstract ones are predominantly feminine or masculine. The masculine abstract nouns tend to represent more aggressive characteristics, whereas the feminine ones tend to suggest a greater degree of submission.[62]

- o die Armut (poverty)
- o die Demut (humbleness)
- o die Langmut (patience)
- o die Sanftmut (meekness)
- o die Schwermut (gloom)
- o die Wehmut (melancholy)

but:

- o der Mut (courage)
- o der Freimut (frankness)
- o der Hochmut (arrogance)
- o der Missmut (displeasure)
- o der Übermut (cockiness)
- o der Unmut (resentment)
- o der Wagemut (daring)

Nouns describing the physical world tend to be neuter, hence *das Bismut* (a chemical element).

Double consonants

Nouns ending on a double consonant can be masculine, neuter or feminine. A combination of Rules 1 and 2 sometimes helps to unlock their gender. Thus, short, single-syllable nouns tend to be masculine, unless they refer to a noun associated with a typical ending for another gender or if they refer to a category of nouns that tends to be of another gender.

Masculine: der Ball, der Drall, der Drill, der Fall, der Hall, der Müll, der Zoll, der Griff, der Stoff, der Damm, der Schlamm, der Sinn, der Tipp, der Biss, der Griess, der Gruss, der Fluss, der Frass (crummy food), der Fuss, der Kloss, der Kuss, der Pass, der Russ, der Spass, der Schweiss, der Spiess, der Strauss, der Schluss, der Schuss, der Stoss, der Schoss, der Fleiss, der Ritt, der Tritt

Neuter: das Ass (ace), das Fass (barrel), das Kinn (chin), das Fell (animal skin), das Schiff (same category as *das Boot*), das Kaff, das Bett, das Brett, das Fett (nouns ending on -*ett* tend to be neuter 95 per cent of the time), das Lamm (diminutives tend to be neuter), das Schloss, das Mass, das Floss, das Gefäss, das Gesäss, das Geschoss (words starting with *Ge-* tend to be neuter), das Edelweiss (the ending is a colour, and colours tend to be neuter)

Feminine: die Nuss (fruit and nuts tend to be feminine), die Null (numbers are feminine), die Nachtigall (smaller birds tend to be feminine), die Geiss (goat)

Nouns with more than one gender

A tiny fraction of German nouns can be mapped to more than one gender. This phenomenon is sometimes caused by regional preferences. For example, if you come from northern Germany, the preference is for *E-Mail* to be feminine because it comes from the same category as *die Post*. In contrast, in southern Germany, Austria and Switzerland, they have concluded that it is an imported foreign word, and accordingly use *das E-Mail*.[63]

Another example is the noun *App*. Some people think that a software app is feminine because it is the abbreviation for *die Applikation*; others think it is neuter because it is part of the same category as *das Programm*. Hence, it is either *die* App or *das* App.

Given that language is dynamic, there will inevitably be shifts in gender over time. For example, the *Duden Fremdwörterbuch* made 199 changes to the gender of nouns between its 1960 and 1997 editions.[64]

The most common combination of genders is masculine and neuter. The neuter option can often be explained by the noun having been imported from another language:

o der/das Aquädukt (imported from Latin, which would tend to make it neuter)
o der/das Barock (referring to Baroque art or music or the age; an imported French word, which should tend to make it neuter)
o der/das Biotop (an imported Greek word, which would typically make it neuter)
o der/das Bonbon (imported from French)

- o der/das Dotter (egg yolk; another word for *das Eigelb*, suggesting a category preference for neuter)
- o der/das Drittel (the Germans say *das*, the Swiss *der*)
- o der/das Dschungel (same category as *der Urwald*, but also a foreign import from jungle, hence, *das*)
- o der/das Extrakt (same as *der Auszug* and *das Konzentrat*)
- o der/das Fakt (from *das Faktum*)
- o der/das Gelee
- o der/das Iglu
- o der/das Indigo
- o der/das Joga/Yoga
- o der/das Kehricht
- o der/das Kosovo (an unusual case of a country with two genders; see also "Oman" below)
- o der/das Liter (the Swiss prefer *der*)
- o der/das Link
- o der/das Log-in/Login
- o der/das Match (the Germans use *das*, because it is a synonym of *das Spiel*; the Swiss *der* because it also means *der Wettkampf*)
- o der/das Marzipan (typically *das*, but in Austria can also be *der*)
- o der/das Meter
- o der/das Nougat/Nugat
- o der/das Oman (*der* preferred in Austria, Switzerland and southern Germany)
- o der/das Perron
- o der/das Piment
- o der/das Pontifikat
- o der/das Purpur (crimson/purple)
- o der/das Pyjama (the Germans prefer *der*, because it is the synonym of *der Schlafanzug*; the Austrians and Swiss prefer *das*, because nouns ending on -*ma* tend to be neuter)
- o der/das Radio (southern Germany, Austria and Switzerland tending to go for *der* because it is in the same category as *der Rundfunk*)
- o der/das Scan

- o der/das Silo
- o der/das Spagat
- o der/das Storno
- o der/das Tattoo
- o der/das Teil (*der Teil* = an integral part of a whole, as in *der Stadtteil*; *das Teil* = a loose piece of something, even if it was once part of a whole; synonymous with *das Stück*)
- o der/das Techno
- o der/das Terminal
- o der/das Thermometer (the Austrians and Swiss go for *der* because of the link to *der Meter*, but the Germans use *das* because the units measuring temperature are neuter, as in *das Celsius, das Fahrenheit, das Kelvin*)
- o der/das Thermostat
- o der/das Viadukt
- o der/das Virus (in technical, scientific use the preference is for *das*)
- o der/das Volleyball

In second place is the combination of masculine/feminine:

- o der/die Abscheu (meaning disgust, revulsion; this word has its roots in *die Scheu*, shyness. Originally, though, *Abscheu* tended to be masculine, which shows how the gender of some words can also shift across the centuries)
- o der/die Fussel (fluff on clothing)
- o der/die Mambo (Latin American dance; dances tend to be masculine)
- o der/die Oblast (oblast)
- o der/die Python (while nouns ending on *-on* tend to be masculine, a python is in the same category as *die Schlange*)
- o der/die Samba (Latin American dance; the ending *-a* is more typical for feminine nouns, but dances tend to be a masculine category)
- o der/die Salbei (sage, the plant/herb; spices tend to be masculine, but the *-ei* ending tends to be feminine)

o der/die Sellerie (vegetables tend to be a masculine categorie if they don't end on -*e*)

Then comes the combination of feminine and neuter:

o die/das Aerobic (*die Übung* or *das Fitnesstraining*)
o die App (die Applikation), das App (das Programm)
o die Cola (northern Germany) or *das Cola* (in Austria, Switzerland and southern Germany)
o die/das Consommé (imported French word, but ending on an -*e* that is associated with feminine nouns)
o die E-Mail (northern Germany) or *das E-Mail* (in Austria, Switzerland and southern Germany)
o die/das Foto (either because the original noun is *die Fotografie* or because nouns ending on -*o* tend to be neuter)
o die/das Furore (imported from the Italian, which would tend to make it neuter, but it has an -*e* ending, which is overwhelmingly associated with feminine nouns)
o die/das SMS (Germans prefer *die*, because SMS is a synonym for *die Kurznachricht*, whereas the Austrians and the Swiss prefer *das*, because imported nouns tend to be neuter)
o die/das Tram (in most of Germany they seem to believe that *Tram* is short for *die Trambahn*, which would make it feminine, but in parts of southern Germany and in Switzerland they believe its origin is a foreign word, tram-car or tramway, and so they went for neuter)

There are very few nouns with three genders:

o der/die/das Bookmark
o der/die/das Dingsbums (watchamacallit/thingamajig)
o der/die/das Joghurt
o der/die/das Spam
o der/die/das Triangel

Note that, occasionally, a different gender for the same noun can change its meaning completely, in which case you do need to know the precise gender. Fortunately, there are only very few such nouns:

o der Appendix (when referring to a book), die Appendix (when referring to anatomy)
o der Band (hardcover book), die Band (music group), das Band (tape)
o der Katarakt (waterfall), die Katarakt (cataract)
o der Kiwi (bird), die Kiwi (fruit)
o der Kristall (the mineral), das Kristall (an article made from crystal glass)
o der Lama (buddhist priest), das Lama (animal)
o das Laster (vice), der Laster (truck)
o der Mast (mast), die Mast (the act of fattening things up)
o der Moment (moment/instant/split second), das Moment (momentum/torque/factor)
o die See (sea), der See (lake)
o das Tor (a big gate, door or goal), der Tor (a fool)
o der Verdienst (earnings), das Verdienst (merit)

Nouns with no gender

There are very few nouns that don't have a gender. They include:

o Aids
o Allerheiligen (All Saints' Day; the First of November in Western Europe)

Not using the grammatical gender because a noun has no gender is not the same as knowing when to omit the definite article in cases where a noun does have a gender. Fortunately, the principles that determine when to omit the definite article are similar in English and German. Just as one can say "I want water", without the definite article, so, too, one would omit the *das* before *Wasser* in German. The same is true when using collective nouns or when generalizing, for example, in the phrase "Wisdom is required". It is only when we want to be very specific, that we add the definite article: "The wisdom of Solomon is required" or "I want the cold water". It is the same in German: *der*, *die*, *das* add precision.

Index and Proficiency Test

To unlock the gender of German nouns, you need to know the gender associated with certain *categories* and *sounds*. This index can, therefore, also serve as a self-test of your proficiency. Each entry essentially requires an answer to the question: "Which gender does this tend to represent?"

differences in gender
  between north and south
  Germany, 129
diminutives, 34, 94
dirt & waste, 20

E

-e, 74
-ee, 77
-eer, 120
-eg, 32
-ei/-erei, 79
-eil, 100
-eis, 32
-el, 41
-em, 100
-en, 32
-ent, 35
-enz, 81
equipment/instruments/tools,
  22
-er, 37
-ett, 101
-euer, 102
-eur, 45

F

-falt, 81
flowers, 71
-fon/-phon, 102
form and shape, 67
fractions, 95
fruit, 71
-ft, 85

G

Ge-, 102

gestures, 70
-gion, 87
-grafie/graphie, 82
-gramm, 106
grammatical terms, 92

H

heavenly bodies, 20
-heit, 82
-horn, 106
human and animal babies, 94
hunting, 69

I

-ial, 106
-ich, 46
-icht, 82
-ie, 83
-iel, 106
-ier, 107
-ig, 47
-ik, 83
-iker, 38, 47
-in, 83
inanimate objects, 12
-ing, 107
inland bodies of water, 20
insects, 71
-ip, 108
-isch, 121
-ismus, 49
-itis/-tis, 84
-iv, 108

J

juices, 22

Notes

[1] Based on an analysis of the around 100,000 nouns listed in the *Duden - Deutsches Universalwörterbuch*, as of mid-2015. Source: *Duden - Deutsches Universalwörterbuch.*

[2] Based on a computer analysis of around 16 million words (i.e. words repeated with all their possible cases) that constituted the Duden German language database, as of mid-2015. Source: *Duden - Deutsches Universalwörterbuch.*

[3] A case in point is the 400-page German grammar book for English students, *A Practice Grammar of German*, by Dreyer and Schmitt (2010). At the very beginning of that book is the advice not to try and learn gender rules, but to "memorize the definite article with each noun".

[4] Twain, Mark. 1880. "The Awful German Language", Appendix D in *A Tramp Abroad*, Chatto & Windus.

[5] Köpcke, Klaus-Michael. 1982. *Untersuchungen zum Genussystem der deutschen Gegenwartssprache.* Max Niemeyer Verlag, page 1. This author cites four language experts of the time, to back up his claim.

[6] Köpcke, Klaus-Michael. 1982. *Untersuchungen zum Genussystem der deutschen Gegenwartssprache.* Max Niemeyer Verlag. Köpcke also worked closely with David Zubin, and they jointly published numerous studies, including Köpcke, Klaus-Michael and Zubin, David A., "Sechs Prinzipien für die Genuszuweisung im Deutschen: Ein Beitrag zur natürlichen Klassifikation" in *Linguistische Berichte* 93 (1984), pp. 26-50, reproduced in Sieburg, Heinz (ed.) 1997. *Sprache – Genus/Sexus.* Peter Lang. See also Zubin, D. A., & Köpcke, K.-M. 1981. Gender: A less than arbitrary grammatical category, in R. A. Hendrick, C. A. Masek, & M. F. Miller (eds.), *Papers from the seventeenth regional meeting, Chicago Linguistic Society* (pp. 439-449). Chicago: Chicago Linguistic Society; Zubin, D. A., and Köpcke, K.-M. 1984. Affect classification in the German gender system. *Lingua*, 63: pp. 41–96; Zubin, D. A., & Köpcke, K.-M. 1986. "Gender and folk-taxonomy: The indexical relation between grammatical gender and lexical categorization", in C. Craik (ed.), *Noun classes and categorization* (pp. 139-180).

[7] The source for the ages by which German children master aspects of German gender, as cited in this paragraph, comes from the studies referenced in Mills, A.E. 1986. *The Acquisition of Gender: A Study of English and German.* Springer-Verlag.

[8] Krohn, Dieter and Krohn Karin. 2008. *Der, das, die - oder wie? Studien zum Genuserwerb schwedischer Deutschlerner.* Peter Lang., p. 107. Köpcke, Klaus-Michael. January 2009. *Genus,* p. 137, references the findings of four separate such experiments.

[9] Exceptions can often be explained by knowledge of other categories, or by a reference to sounds (Rule 2). See, for example, the chapter on neuter nouns for an explanation of why it is *das Bier* and *das Wasser.*

[10] For example, the imported word "Blockchain" is feminine because a German noun for "chain" already exists, and it is feminine: die Kette.

[11] Source: *Duden - Deutsches Universalwörterbuch* (as of mid-2015).

[12] The source for the ages by which German children master aspects of German gender, as cited in this paragraph, comes from the studies referenced in Mills, A.E. 1986. *The Acquisition of Gender: A Study of English and German.* Springer-Verlag.

[13] See the Greek and Latin text in Brugmann, Karl. 1889. "Das Nominalgeschlecht in den Indogermanischen Sprachen", in *Techmers Internationaler Zeitschrift für allgemeine Sprachwissenschaft,* 4 (1889), pp. 100-109, reproduced in Sieburg, Heinz (ed.) 1997. *Sprache – Genus/Sexus.* Peter Lang, pp. 33-43.

[14] This hypothesis is discussed in Köpcke, Klaus-Michael and Zubin, David A., "Sechs Prinzipien für die Genuszuweisung im Deutschen: Ein Beitrag zur natürlichen Klassifikation" in *Linguistische Berichte* 93 (1984), pp. 26-50, reproduced in Sieburg, Heinz (ed.) 1997. *Sprache – Genus/Sexus.* Peter Lang, pp. 101-107.

[15] These percentages are derived from Table 2.7 "Some Phonetic Rules of Gender Assignment in German", in Mills, A.E. 1986. *The Acquisition of Gender: A Study of English and German.* Springer-Verlag., p. 33.

[16] Köpcke, Klaus-Michael. 1982. *Untersuchungen zum Genussystem der deutschen Gegenwartssprache*; Köpcke, Klaus-Michael. 1994.

[17] Instead of associating *das Atelier* as being in the same category as *das Haus*, one might have associated it with *die Wohnung,* which is also a reasonable association to make. But that would have required you to ignore the *-ier* ending, which tends to signal neuter, especially if you recognized the noun as an imported French word.

[18] This hypothesis is discussed in Köpcke, Klaus-Michael and Zubin, David A., "Sechs Prinzipien für die Genuszuweisung im Deutschen: Ein Beitrag zur natürlichen Klassifikation" in *Linguistische Berichte* 93 (1984), pp. 26-50, reproduced in Sieburg, Heinz (ed.) 1997. *Sprache – Genus/Sexus*. Peter Lang, pp. 97-98.

[19] There is, however, a trend towards looking for creative ways to avoid needlessly specifying the gender associated with roles and functions. A similar trend is to be found in English, where we see fewer references to "his or her" and more use of the plural form "their". Whereas English has far fewer cases where a noun ending identifies the gender of the person (as in "actors and actresses"), the German language is littered with such duplications. Accordingly, the following tricks are used in German: Instead of referring to "Studentinnen und Studenten", for example, one now finds the term "Studierende", which means "those who are studying" – a gender-free phrase. Another creative way to try and get around identifying the gender is to reformulate the sentence from the active tense to the passive tense. For example, instead of saying that "Actors and actresses will receive their royalties at the end of the year", one could just say: "Royalties will be distributed at the end of the year." Looking for creative ways to use this shortened form of language also means that it must be obvious from the context who one is referring to.

[20] Here we have another relatively rare case where synonyms of closely-related nouns do not share the same gender: While it is *der Swimmingpool*, it is *das Schwimmbad.*

[21] Given that nouns ending with *-horn* tend to be neuter, we have *das Matterhorn*. Similarly, given that nouns ending on *-e* are overwhelmingly feminine, it should be no surprise to find mountains ending on *-e* being feminine too, e.g. *die Wildspitze.*

[22] See the entry for nouns ending on -ier in the chapter on neuter nouns for an explanation of why it is *das Bier*.

[23] It can also be *der/die Mambo, der/die Rumba, der/die Samba*.

[24] Imported from English, which should tend to make *Gag* neuter, but here we have an example of how the *-ag* ending has helped to make it a masculine noun: *der Gag*. Another example is *der Lag*, from the English noun lag; the *-ag* ending is strongly masculine, therefore.

[25] See the entry for "countries" in the chapter on neuter nouns for an explanation of when to show the article *das* when referring to a neuter country, because the article is usually omitted.

[26] In Austria, it can also be referred to as *der Marzipan*.

[27] Nouns starting with *Ge-* are overwhelmingly neuter, but here is a rare exception where the *-ang* ending helps to make it masculine. That would suggest that *-ang* is a strong masculine ending.

[28] When this noun is feminine (*die Mast*), it refers to food-related concepts, in a similar category as *die Nahrung, die Speise, die Kost*.

[29] Imported nouns tend to be neuter or allocated to the gender of their German synonym. The noun *der Toast* meets neither of these rules if it refers to toasted bread, but its gender is consistent with the synomym *der Trinkspruch,* in the sense of raising one's glass in honour of someone.

[30] Wegener, Heide. 1995. *Die Nominalflexion des Deutschen – verstanden als Lerngegenstand.* Max Niemeyer Verlag., p. 75.

[31] ibid., p. 75.

[32] In German, one can identify a verb in the infinitive form by its *-en* ending, as in *spielen* (to play*)*. Now let's turn *spielen* into a noun. If you wanted to refer to "the act of playing", in the sense of "playing is an important activity in kindergarten", then you would capitalize *Spielen* to show that it has become a noun. Nouns that have been created from verbs in this way are typically neuter: *das Spielen*. This rule allows you to know the gender of many nouns created in this way. Similarly, if you come across a noun ending on *-en* that was clearly not derived from a verb, such as in the case of *Kindergarten* (clearly not a verb), then the

probability is high that the noun is masculine, because the majority of nouns that end in -*en* that are not derived from verbs are masculine, hence *der Kindergarten.*

[33] Nouns ending on -*ment* tend to be neuter; see the chapter on neuter nouns.

[34] For details on -*ier* endings, see the chapter on neuter nouns.

[35] Wegener, Heide. *op. cit.*, p. 75.

[36] ibid., p. 75.

[37] If *Butter* seems like it should be masculine, in parts of southwestern Germany it is in some dialects. Source: Bastian Sick, *Zwiebelfisch*, "Der Butter, die Huhn, das Teller", www.Spiegel.de, 23 August 2006.

[38] Wegener, Heide. *op. cit.*, p. 75.

[39] ibid., p. 75.

[40] ibid., p. 75.

[41] Nouns ending on -*ur* tend to be feminine; see the -*ur* entry in the chapter on feminine nouns.

[42] The percentages for -*ich* nouns has been derived from Table 2.7 "Some Phonetic Rules of Gender Assignment in German", in Mills, A.E. 1986. *The Acquisition of Gender: A Study of English and German.* Springer-Verlag., p. 33.

[43] Köpcke, Klaus-Michael. 1982. *Untersuchungen zum Genussystem der deutschen Gegenwartssprache.* Max Niemeyer Verlag.

[44] See the -*ing* entry in the chapter on neuter nouns.

[45] See, for example, Köpcke, Klaus-Michael. 1982. *Untersuchungen zum Genussystem der deutschen Gegenwartssprache* and *Köpcke, Klaus-Michael. January 2009. Genus*, p. 136, which references further bibliography on this topic.

[46] Not the same meaning or gender as *das Wort.*

[47] Some exceptions: *das Klavier*, because nouns of inanimate objects ending on *-ier* tend to be neuter, as in *das Bier, das Papier*; this also means the the synonym of *Klavier, das Piano*, will be neuter. In the case of *Saxophon*, nouns ending on Greek roots, as in the case of *phon*, would tend to be neuter.

[48] Discussed in Köpcke, Klaus-Michael and Zubin, David A., "Sechs Prinzipien für die Genuszuweisung im Deutschen: Ein Beitrag zur natürlichen Klassifikation" in *Linguistische Berichte* 93 (1984), pp. 26-50, reproduced in Sieburg, Heinz (ed.) 1997. *Sprache – Genus/Sexus*. Peter Lang, pp. 97-98.

[49] This percentage comes from Table 2.7 "Some Phonetic Rules of Gender Assignment in German", in Mills, A.E. 1986. *The Acquisition of Gender: A Study of English and German.* Springer-Verlag., p. 33.

[50] Wegener, Heide. *op. cit.*, p. 75.

[51] ibid., p. 75.

[52] See the entry "units of measurement of temperature" in the chapter on neuter nouns.

[53] This percentage comes from Table 2.7 "Some Phonetic Rules of Gender Assignment in German", in Mills, A.E. 1986. *The Acquisition of Gender: A Study of English and German.* Springer-Verlag., p. 33.

[54] The percentages for *-cht* nouns have been derived from Table 2.7 "Some Phonetic Rules of Gender Assignment in German", in Mills, A.E. 1986. *The Acquisition of Gender: A Study of English and German.* Springer-Verlag., p. 33.

[55] Nouns ending on *-eur* are typically masculine if they refer to a profession, role or activity. For more details, see the *-eur* entry in the chapter on masculine nouns.

[56] The percentages for *-ur and -ür* nouns have been derived from Table 2.7 "Some Phonetic Rules of Gender Assignment in German", in Mills, A.E. 1986. *The Acquisition of Gender: A Study of English and German.* Springer-Verlag., p. 33.

[57] According to an internet search conducted in mid-2017, there was a 6:4 preference for *der* Kosovo over *das* Kosovo.

[58] But curiously, not *der Welpe* (puppy/young dog).

[59] The percentages for *-ett* nouns has been derived from Table 2.7 "Some Phonetic Rules of Gender Assignment in German", in Mills, A.E. 1986. *The Acquisition of Gender: A Study of English and German.* Springer-Verlag., p. 33.

[60] The percentages for *-ier* nouns have been derived from Table 2.7 "Some Phonetic Rules of Gender Assignment in German", in Mills, A.E. 1986. *The Acquisition of Gender: A Study of English and German.* Springer-Verlag., p. 33.

[61] It can also be *die Foto*, because the original word was *die Fotografie*.

[62] This hypothesis is discussed in Köpcke, Klaus-Michael and Zubin, David A., "Sechs Prinzipien für die Genuszuweisung im Deutschen: Ein Beitrag zur natürlichen Klassifikation" in *Linguistische Berichte* 93 (1984), pp. 26-50, reproduced in Sieburg, Heinz (ed.) 1997. *Sprache – Genus/Sexus.* Peter Lang, pp. 101-107.

[63] In German, the correct spelling of *E-Mail* still requires a hyphen between the "E" and the "M", and both need to be capitalized. If you were to leave out the hyphen and keep the "m" small, then you have the German noun for something very different – "enamel".

[64] Schulte-Beckhausen, Marion. 2001. *Genusschwankung bei englischen, französischen, italienischen und spanischen Lehnwörtern im Deutschen: Eine Untersuchung auf der Grundlage deutscher Wörterbücher seit 1945.* Verlag Peter Lang, p. 223. While it may come as a surprise that some German nouns have actually changed their gender over the centuries, let's not forget that even humans can be reclassified in terms of gender. In 2018, Germany amended its laws to add a third gender for humans. Birth certificates now also offer the category "divers", an adjective meaning "varied/more than one". Source: Deutscher Bundestag. 2018. *Bundestag erlaubt im Geburtenregister die Bezeichnung „divers".* https://www. bundestag.de/dokumente/textarchiv/2018/kw48-pa-inneres-geburtenregister/578572

Made in the USA
Las Vegas, NV
24 September 2022

55909392R00090